A-Z of Challenging Behaviour Series

S FOR SCHOOL REFUSAL BEHAVIOUR:
POSITIVE BEHAVIOUR SUPPORT

Dolly Bhargava

Master of Special Education

Copyright © 2020 Behaviour Help Pty Ltd. The contents of this guide (text and graphics) are protected by international copyright law. No part of this publication may be reproduced, stored in a retrieval system, transmitted, broadcast or communicated in any form or by any means, optical, digital, electronic, mechanical, photocopying, recording or otherwise, without written permission of Behaviour Help. To obtain permission, email: admin@behaviourhelp.com

Behaviour data collection forms can be reproduced with citation: Bhargava, D. (2020). S for School Refusal Behaviour: Positive Behaviour Support. Melbourne, Vic: Behaviour Help Pty Ltd.

Please note the word 'child' in this guide refers to children of all ages (primary and high school). The information set out in this guide is of a general nature only and not exhaustive on the subject matter. You should consider whether the information is appropriate to the needs of the child you support and your circumstances. This guide should not be used as a diagnostic tool. When implementing any recommendations contained in this guide, exercise independent skill and judgement. If you have any concerns about your child's behaviours, please discuss them with a doctor who can provide guidance and/or a referral to the relevant professional.

A - Z of Challenging Behaviours Series

Titles

A for Argumentative

A for Attention-Seeking

B for Biting

C for Cheating

D for Defiance

E for Excessive Reassurance Seeking

E for Excessive Technology Use

F for Flopping

H for Hitting

I for Impulsivity

K for Kicking

L for Lying

R for Repetitive Questioning

S for School Refusal Behaviour

S for Separation Anxiety

S for Stealing

T for Task Avoidance

The list of titles is being expanded all the time. For the latest, please refer to www.behaviourhelp.com

ACKNOWLEDGEMENTS

I wish to thank the following people for helping me put this series together despite COVID-19 restrictions.

My husband and children – Gaj, Navina and Ethan
My beyond amazing editor - Keith Ougden

CONTENTS

1. PREFACE 1
2. INTRODUCTION TO SCHOOL REFUSAL BEHAVIOUR 3
3. DEFINING POSITIVE BEHAVIOUR SUPPORT 6
4. ASSESS-MANAGE-PREVENT STAGES 11
5. ASSESS STAGE 15
6. MANAGE STAGE 45
7. PREVENT STAGE 65
8. CONCLUSION 85
9. REFERENCES 86
APPENDIX: BEHAVIOUR HELP WEB-BASED APP 90
ABOUT THE AUTHOR 92

1. PREFACE

All children experience difficulties with managing their emotions and behaviours at one time or another. With understanding, support and encouragement, most children learn the skills they need to manage this. However, some children repeatedly engage in emotional and behavioural responses that can cause serious harm to others and/or themselves. Despite best efforts and intentions, the child has difficulties learning how to manage their emotions and behaviours and the situation does not appear to improve.

As a parent, caregiver, educator, support staff or professional, facing the child's challenging emotional and behavioural responses daily can result in feeling stress, exhausted and disheartened. If any of this sounds familiar, then this guide will provide a roadmap developed from the evidenced-based approach of Positive Behaviour Support (PBS) to help guide the child to learn positive ways of behaving and managing their emotions.

S for School Refusal Behaviour (SRB) recognises SRB as a complex behaviour with multiple factors contributing to its development and persistence. While schools cannot address all the factors that contribute to the SRB outside of their environment, they can play an important role in contributing to the re-entry plan that promotes and supports the child's school attendance on a part-time or full-time basis.

Utilising the PBS approach this guide includes many detailed and practical ideas to develop a comprehensive PBS plan by guiding the reader through the three distinct stages of PBS:

- ASSESS: How to identify the triggers (events) related to school that contribute to challenging behaviours related to school refusal,
- MANAGE: How to respond and support the child when they are triggered at school, and
- PREVENT: How to minimise or avoid the triggers at school.

The guide contains practical tools (forms, checklists and strategies) to assist the process of developing a PBS plan. The forms are available as a free download in the Free Resources section of www.behaviourhelp.com. The website also includes access to the web-based Behaviour Help app http://www.behaviourhelp.com/app/#/signup. The app can be used to systematically assess incidents of challenging behaviour and develop individualised behaviour management and prevention plans.

Please remember, it is never too late to change a behaviour. Change does not happen overnight; instead it is a process that takes time. Change is also not a straightforward process. Instead it is like a rollercoaster where there are ups and downs, moves forward, moves backwards and then forward again. The key is that with persistence, patience and perseverance the child can gradually learn positive ways of behaving and managing their emotions.

I would like to take this opportunity to commend you for taking a step in this journey to make a difference and create a better future for your child.

Best wishes,
Dolly Bhargava

2. INTRODUCTION TO SCHOOL REFUSAL BEHAVIOUR

Most children have occasional days when they do not want to go to school because they're worried about something, such as a test, participating in a swimming carnival or seeing a peer they had an argument with the previous day. When this happens, families can help their child by talking through the issues, encouraging them or letting them have a rare day off school.

Usually, the reluctance or refusal to go to school will fade; however, some children show a repetitive and persistent pattern of reluctance or refusal to attend school. Terms used to describe this behaviour include absenteeism, truancy and School Refusal Behaviour (SRB).

Absenteeism is when a child regularly misses school, usually with caregiver knowledge and consent. A child might be absent because of health issues, unstable housing or transportation, bullying, fear of violence, difficulties with learning or keeping up with homework or assessment tasks (Allison & Attisha, 2019).

Truancy is when a child misses class or school without caregiver knowledge and consent and leaves school early intentionally without permission (Barry, Chaney & Chaney, 2011; Henry & Thornberry, 2010). Children who truant are usually not anxious or fearful about attending school, engage in antisocial behaviour often in the company of antisocial peers, lack interest or willingness to do school work, do not conform to the school's codes of conduct, and during school hours are not at home (Kearney, 2008; & Sewell, 2008).

School Refusal Behaviour (SRB) is when a child or adolescent shows reluctance or refusal to remain in class all day or attend school on an ongoing basis (Lyon & Colter, 2007; Heyne et al., 2019; & Sewell, 2008). Caregivers are aware that their child is staying home from school over a prolonged period of time. SRB is seen in children and adolescents aged between 5 and 17 (Kearney, Cook, & Chapman, 2007).

SRB is frequently accompanied by various other diagnoses and is seen as a symptom associated with these diagnoses. For example, social anxiety disorder, generalised anxiety disorder, specific phobia, major depression, oppositional defiant disorder, post-traumatic stress disorder and adjustment disorder (Kawsar, Yilanli & Marwaha, 2020).

SRB is associated with emotional distress and can show itself behaviourally, physiologically and cognitively.

- Behavioural symptoms may start the night before or in the morning before school and may include a child refusing to leave their bed, locking themselves in their bedroom or begging not to go to school; sometimes this can escalate to screaming or having temper tantrums. If the child does eventually go to school, they may be late, refuse to leave the car, be excessively clingy to their parent or repeatedly ask to go home. They may need a lot of encouragement to get them through the school gates. Once they are in school, they might spend long periods out of their classroom – for example they might be in the principal's office or sick bay – or they might repeatedly ask to call home, leave school early or even run away from school.
- Physiological symptoms may include being dizzy, sweating a lot, having headaches, being shaky or trembly, having heart palpitations or chest pains, having a stomach ache, feeling sick (or actually being sick), needing the toilet frequently or just generally having aches and pains.
- Cognitive symptoms include being overly worried or having irrational thoughts about school (for example, worrying about tests, speaking in front of the class or having to interact with other children), being concerned about being separated from parents and/or pets, or other general concerns like having their things stolen while they are at school (Fremont, 2003; Heyne et al., 2001; & Tonge et al., 2002).

SRB takes a heavy toll on the child, causes distress to the family, and presents a challenge to the school and professionals (Heyne, et al., 2002).

Kearney and Silverman (1996) identified a continuum of school refusal behaviours that can be used to understand the stages of its presentation:

- Marked distress on school days and pleading with caregivers to stay home, but school attendance is achieved through encouragement.
- Repeated misbehaviours such as tantrums or clinginess before attending school.
- Repeated tardiness such as dawdling or running away from the car in the morning before attending school.
- Periodic absences or skipping classes.
- Repeated absences or skipping of classes mixed with attendance.
- Complete absence from school during a certain period of the school year.
- Complete absence from school for a year or more.

When SRB is prolonged and ongoing, it becomes ingrained in the child. Setzer and Salhauer (2001) use the following descriptors to identify the severity and the chronicity of the various types of SRB:

- Initial SRB: Lasts for a brief period (less than two weeks) and may resolve without intervention.
- Substantial SRB: Lasts for a minimum of two weeks and requires some form of intervention.
- Acute SRB: Lasts for two weeks to one year, being a consistent problem for a majority of the time.
- Chronic SRB: Interferes or overlaps with two or more academic years.

Short-term impacts for the child include poor academic performance, family difficulties, difficulties with maintaining friendships, problems with peers, and increased risk of legal trouble which can lead to longer-term consequences (Kearney, 2001; Wijetunge & Lakmini, 2011). Long-term consequences include social isolation, academic underachievement, employment issues, increased risk of mental health problems and developing a psychiatric illness in adulthood, such as panic disorder and agoraphobia (Fremont, 2003; Flakierska-Praquin et al, 1997 and Sewell, 2008).

For the family, the resulting cumulative stress from supporting a child with SRB can lead to familial conflict, disrupted routines, increased financial expense and increased potential for poor supervision or child maltreatment (Kearney, 2001).

For the school, SRB presents a challenge and causes frustration. Therefore, it is vital that SRB is addressed as early as possible and that home and school work together to support the child.

3. DEFINING POSITIVE BEHAVIOUR SUPPORT

Positive Behaviour Support (PBS) is an evidence-based approach that is used to eliminate or minimise the occurrence of challenging behaviours. "Challenging behaviour is any behaviour that interferes with children's learning, development, success at play; is harmful to the child, other children or adults; and puts them at high risk for later social problems or school failure" (Klass, Guskin & Thomas, 1995, p. 5). Examples of challenging behaviours include aggressive behaviours, destructive behaviours, inappropriate social behaviours, self-injurious and withdrawn behaviours. In this guide, challenging behaviours related to school refusal within the school context, will be addressed by utilising the PBS approach to enhance the child's communication and social, emotional, behavioural and learning outcomes.

PBS recognises that SRB is a complex problem with multiple factors contributing to its development and persistence. Risk factors are associated with the child, family, peers, school and community (Kearney, 2008).

Child-related factors that increase the risk of the development of SRB include:

- Children who have internalising problems (e.g., anxiety, depression, withdrawal and loneliness) and externalising problems (e.g. aggression, oppositional behaviour and defiance)
- Children in out-of-home care or affected by homelessness
- Children from an Indigenous background
- Children who are young parents and/or carers
- Children who abuse drugs and alcohol
- Children with developmental disabilities (e.g. Autism Spectrum Disorder, Intellectual Disability and Attention Deficit Hyperactivity Disorder)
- Children with chronic health issues

- (e.g. Encopresis (bowel incontinence) and Enuresis (bed-wetting))
- Children experiencing bullying
- Children with learning disabilities (e.g. Dyslexia, Dysgraphia and Dyscalculia)
- Children from families where there is disharmony, dysfunction and poor parental practices
- Children who have experienced trauma
- Children from a refugee background

Family-related factors that contribute to SRB include:

- Caregiver with mental health issues (e.g. Depression, panic disorder and agoraphobia (fear of leaving the home))
- Caregiver with drug/alcohol problems
- Caregiver attitudes and responses to a child's SRB (e.g. child is allowed to engage in preferred activities, such as spending time on technology or games, going shopping or travelling with the caregiver; caregiver encouraging the child to stay at home so they can look after the siblings)
- Characteristics of the family (e.g. parental separation/divorce; abuse and neglect; financial difficulties affecting purchase of school-related items and/or transportation to school)
- Unstable living arrangements (e.g. living in more than one home or temporary accommodation)

School-related factors that contribute to SRB include:

- Moving to a new school
- Returning to school after a long absence
- Problems with teachers
- Difficulties with curriculum
- Changes to routines and staff

Peer-related factors that contribute to SRB include:

- Association with antisocial, truant or delinquent peers
- Social rejection
- Social isolation
- Bullying or conflict with peers

(Gubbels et al., 2019; McShane et al., 2001; Heyne et al., 2002; Kearney, 2008).

The following case study emphasises this complexity:

When John was six years old, his parents separated. His dad moved interstate, leaving his mum to look after and provide for John and his older brother, who has learning difficulties.

John's mum reported changes she saw in John after the divorce. John went from an outgoing, fun, talkative boy to a quiet, shy and withdrawn child. He developed separation anxiety and would follow her everywhere in the house. He could only have her out of sight for a few minutes before he had to find her. On the way to school, she would have to reassure him repeatedly that she would be picking him up at 3pm. If she was late by a couple of minutes, John would have a meltdown. She could not convince him to go to school camps or sleepovers because he would never sleep away from home. He would always talk about his fears about what would happen to his mum if he wasn't next to her.

She also reflected on how John always had trouble making friends. His peers knew his name and would occasionally greet him but there wasn't anyone he could hang out with at recess or lunch.

In Year 5, his mum noticed John starting to say things like 'I hate school' or 'I don't want to go to school', but with her encouragement, he was able to. She didn't think much of this behaviour as it would happen occasionally, and she was able to manage it.

However, the SRB escalated when John started high school. John's reluctance to go to school started to consistently appear once or twice a week, but John's mum was able to convince John to go to school by offering him money to buy a treat from the canteen or after school.

At the beginning of Year 8, within a few weeks of school resuming, John started to outright refuse to go to school. He told his mother that he felt 'lost', he 'didn't belong at school' and he was 'dumb'. During this period, he also started to ask questions about why his dad left and why his dad had not been in touch for the last seven years.

John's mum could see her son needed help, so she increased the amount of support she was giving him to get to school. She would wake him up in the morning, but that could take up to 30 minutes of going in and out of his bedroom. She would then help him prepare his breakfast, keep prompting him to eat and to get dressed for school. She would then drive him to school even though it was a 10-minute walk from their house. During school, John started to increasingly complain of stomach aches and chest pains by lunchtime and would then stay in the sick bay for the rest of the day where he would play games on his laptop. Despite John's mum's complaints to the school, their limited resources prevented staff from providing consistent additional support to John.

In the meantime, John's mum was offered a permanent job. As the single income earner, John's mum had no choice but to accept the job, which meant she would leave home by 6am and get home at 6pm. She would no longer be able to get John ready for school and drop him off. She helped him set an alarm, but John would still not wake up on time. He started to skip school entirely and stayed at home all day playing video games. This quickly devolved into a habit of playing video games until 3am and sleeping until midday. A whole term of school passed by and John had not been to school.

Knowing she needed to do something, John's mum took him to see a range of professionals. He was diagnosed with Depression, Anxiety (Social anxiety disorder and Separation anxiety disorder) and Autism Spectrum Disorder.

John's case study shows the complex nature of the development and maintenance of SRB. There is no quick fix or magic wand that can address all these issues overnight. John's issues, as with any other child, are so multifaceted that a team approach is necessary to assess the underlying factors contributing to his SRB and develop a plan to manage them.

The above example highlights that there is no single cause for SRB. In a context such as primary and secondary school it is not possible to control all the factors that contribute to the SRB outside of the school context. However, factors specific to the school context such as the environment, activity and interactions can be addressed to help the child achieve better communication, social, emotional, behavioural and learning outcomes.

PBS provides a road map to address SRB by using a holistic approach to develop a comprehensive and individualised PBS plan in three stages: Assess-Manage-Prevent.

4. ASSESS-MANAGE-PREVENT STAGES

PBS involves three stages:

- The Assess stage aims to identify the triggers (events) related to school that contribute to challenging behaviours related to school refusal and understand the purpose (function) of the challenging behaviours related to school refusal. These findings will inform the development of a comprehensive and individualised PBS intervention plan that is based on information gathered from the Manage and Prevent stages.
- The Manage stage aims to provide guidelines to help everyone supporting the child at school to respond, when the child is triggered, in a planned, safe and least disruptive manner.
- The Prevent stage aims to minimise or avoid the triggers at school that contribute to the challenging behaviours related to school refusal by tailoring activities, environments and interactions. The prevent stage also aims to teach the child positive ways of communicating their messages and managing their emotions and behaviours.
- Once the PBS plan is implemented it is important to evaluate the effectiveness of the Manage and Prevent stages by repeating the Assess stage to measure the amount or type of progress that has been made. This can help you determine the effectiveness of the Manage and Prevent strategies and refine and adapt them to ultimately help the child reach their full potential.

'Unity is strength ... when there is teamwork and collaboration, wonderful things can be achieved'.

– Mattie Stepanek

Dealing with a child's behaviours can be extremely stressful, demoralising and disheartening. It is also unlikely that any one person will have all the answers to the challenges. Along with the parents and caregivers, it is useful to identify a team who know the child well. This could include educators, school psychologist, school counsellor, school nurse, school administration staff, professionals, disability support and community staff who can work together for the benefit of the child.

It is crucial that the child has access to relevant professionals depending on their needs. Below are examples of services that professionals can provide.

This may include:

- Psychiatrists - can assess mental and physical symptoms to diagnose mental health conditions, manage treatment and provide a range of therapies for various conditions. They can also prescribe medications if warranted by the severity of symptoms.
- Psychologists - can provide assessment, treatment and therapy for emotional, behavioural and learning difficulties. Psychologists can also provide Cognitive Behaviour Therapy to address the underlying causes of SRB. For example, a psychologist can help the child learn a range of emotional regulation skills to help the child learn how to manage the stress related to situations associated with school attendance (e.g. getting ready to go to school, being around other children at school, staying in class for an entire session, asking for help, taking tests and giving a class presentation). Techniques such as using realistic, practical and healthy ways of thinking about the stressful situation, learning a range of relaxation strategies such as deep breathing, visual imagery, progressive muscle relaxation or listening to music can help the child cope with their emotions. Psychologists can also plan and collaborate with the family to identify the best approach to guide and support their child.
- Allied Health Professionals - are tertiary-qualified health professionals who, through their training, have gained a high level of skill in child development. For example, speech pathologists can assess and provide treatment and therapy for speech, language, social and literacy difficulties the child may have. An occupational therapist can provide assessment, treatment and therapy to help children become independent and address sensory issues.
- Learning specialists-can provide assessment, tutoring and support to children who have academic difficulties.

Each person on the team has their special knowledge and perspective. The school can work in partnership through the assess-manage-prevent stage in a unified way to increase the probability of achieving the best outcome for the child and supporting them to reach their potential.

The first step therefore, depending on the child's needs, is to identify all the people that will be involved in the team. Use the *Team Member Chart* provided on the next page to record the names, roles and contexts in which they support the child.

Team Member Chart

Child name _____

Recorder name _____

Date _____

Team member name	Role	Context where they support the child (e.g. home, day centre, school and therapy)

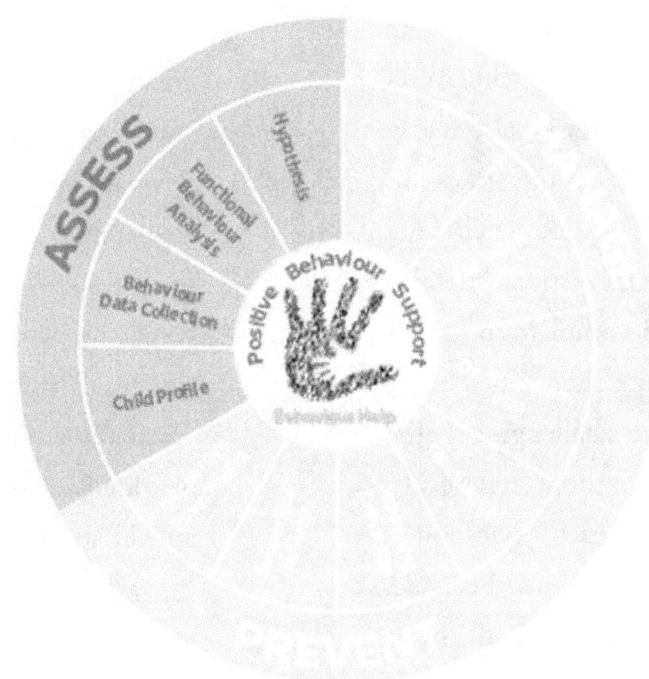

5. ASSESS STAGE

Assessment is the process of understanding the reasons, purpose or function of the challenging behaviours related to school refusal.

The Assess Stage helps to identity:

- School activity related factors which contribute to the challenging behaviours,
- School environment related factors which contribute to the challenging behaviours, and
- School staff and peer related factors which contribute to the challenging behaviours.

To identify these factors, a combination of indirect and direct assessment methods is used.

Assess Stage Checklist:

- Child's profile – Indirect methods include interviews with the child if appropriate and gathering information from people who know the child well such as their caregiver(s), educators and professionals, reviewing any reports, rating scales and checklists. This guide includes a child's profile that various members of the team can complete to gain insight into factors that may be contributing to the challenging behaviours related to school refusal. Explanations why each question is asked is included before the child's profile form. By collating all the information, it will create a comprehensive picture of who the child is, their abilities and needs.

- Behaviour data collection form – This is a direct method and includes observing a child during real time and measuring the challenging behaviour that presents in the school context. Measurable dimensions include frequency (how often it occurs), duration (how long it can last) and intensity (how severe it is). The forms can be used to collate the data over the course of at least a few weeks or longer. Collecting data can help identify and understand any patterns of behaviour.

- Functional Behaviour Analysis (FBA) – This is a direct method that involves reflecting on an incident by answering a series of questions to identify what happened before and after the challenging behaviour. These results can be used to work out what triggered the behaviour and the purpose (function) that the behaviour served. To complete an FBA, use the form provided in this guide or the Behaviour Help web-based app (www.behaviourhelp.com/app/#/sign up).

Child's Profile

To create a comprehensive picture of the child, their abilities and needs the following areas need to be considered. If the child has difficulties in any of these areas, intervention is critical. Without the appropriate supports, services and strategies these unaddressed difficulties can contribute to the child exhibiting SRB.

General health

Health is a state of physical, mental and social well-being that allows the child to adequately cope with demands of daily life. It is important to investigate any health-related issues (e.g. illness, infections, allergies and pain) first, particularly if the behaviour has suddenly become more intense and/or is not responding to trialled behaviour management strategies.

It is also important to record any diagnosis the child has. Diagnosis of conditions describe a broad range of health conditions including:

- Chronic illnesses (e.g. cancer, diabetes and asthma),
- Mental health conditions (e.g. anxiety, depression and schizophrenia),
- Trauma and stress related disorders
- Neurodevelopmental disorders (e.g. autism spectrum disorder, intellectual disability, attention deficit hyperactivity disorder and Down syndrome), communication disorders (e.g. language disorder, stuttering and social/language disorder), motor disorders (e.g. Tourette's disorder, dyspraxia and tic disorder),
- Feeding and eating disorders (e.g. anorexia nervosa, bulimia nervosa or binge eating disorder),
- Elimination disorder (e.g. encopresis, enuresis),
- Sleep-wake disorders (e.g. obstructive sleep apnoea, parasomnias, narcolepsy, and restless leg syndrome),
- Personality disorders (e.g. bipolar personality disorder),
- Substance-related and addictive disorders, and
- Disruptive, impulse-control and conduct disorders (e.g. oppositional defiant disorder, conduct disorder, intermittent explosive disorder, kleptomania and pyromania).

Every child is unique and even children with the same diagnosis will have different abilities, needs and preferences. When completing the profile, it is important to record the impact of the diagnosis on the child's skill development. This will help identify the necessary supports, strategies and services the child needs to reach their full potential.

Information on any medications, alcohol or drugs the child may be consuming needs to be recorded. Any side effects that affect the child's learning (e.g. memory issues), emotions (e.g. irritability), behaviour (e.g. overreaction) and communication need to be understood. Intervention is critical for addressing the child's health needs.

Visual skills

Vision plays an important role in a child's growth, development and daily performance. Disease, damage or injury to any part of the visual system (i.e. eye, visual pathway to the brain or visual centre of the brain) causes a vision impairment which results in reduced visual functioning for learning (Department of Education, 2011). If a child has a vision impairment it is important to determine their unique support needs and determine the best type of assistance. Without the necessary supports it can adversely affect their social, psychological, communication, physical and academic performance (Rainey et. al, 2016) contributing to SRB. Intervention is critical for helping the child develop vision skills.

Hearing skills

Hearing plays an important role in the development of speech and language skills, social interaction skills and daily performance. Hearing impairment or loss occurs when there is a problem with or damage to one or more parts of the hearing mechanism (i.e. one or more parts of the ear or ears, hearing pathway to the brain or the hearing centre of the brain) (Department of Education, 2011). Hearing impairment can impose basic limitations on a child, in terms of access to spoken language, access to environmental auditory experiences and ease of interacting with a wide range of people. These difficulties can lead to learning problems that result in reduced academic achievement, social isolation and poor self-concept contributing to SRB. Intervention is critical for helping the child develop listening skills.

Physical skills

Physical skills are comprised of gross motor skills (e.g. sit, stand and walk) and/or fine motor skills (e.g. eat, write and cut). Gross motor and fine motor skills allow a child to explore and interact with the world around them. When a child has difficulties with these skill sets, it can negatively impact their ability to move or coordinate and control their bodies to perform the skills necessary for accessing, participating in and learning from their environment. These difficulties can lead to learning difficulties, low self-esteem and frustration which contribute to SRB. Intervention is critical for helping the child develop physical skills.

Sensory needs

There are eight types of sensory information that are received by different parts of the body: vision (eyes), auditory/hearing (ears), olfactory/smell (nose), gustatory/taste (tongue), vestibular /balance and movement (inner ears), tactile/touch (skin), proprioception/pressure and body awareness (joints and tendons) and interoception/messages from inside the body (internal organs).

Sensory processing refers to the way the brain receives, processes and organises the information received through the senses and turns them into appropriate motor and behavioural responses. Some children have a Sensory Processing Disorder (SPD). SPD is a neurological condition that means the brain is not able to process and organise the messages received from the senses into appropriate responses.

Children with SPD may show hypersensitivity, where they react too strongly to the sensory information, or hyposensitivity, where they are seemingly unaware of the input. If a child is hyposensitive, they will crave or seek sensory input to keep their bodies calm. If a child is hypersensitive, they will react too strongly to the sensory information.

A child with sensory issues may become overwhelmed by sensory input. For example, a child may experience sensory overload in a classroom if they find it too noisy, too crowded, too visually over-stimulating or not leaving enough personal space which will leave them feeling unsafe and insecure.

To address the child's sensory needs, they need a 'sensory diet' designed by an Occupational Therapist. A 'sensory diet' is a carefully designed, personalised activity plan that provides the right combination of sensory input a child needs to stay alert, engaged, focused and organised throughout the day. Each day depending on the child's needs a sensory diet is created to provide the necessary combinations of sensory input to 'feed or nourish' the child's nervous system at frequent intervals throughout the day to help the child stay regulated (Prizant et al., 2006). Without a sensory diet the child may not receive the necessary sensory input throughout the day and become dysregulated. The SRB may be one of the few tools the child has to express how they are feeling and attempt to gain some form of control in situations that are causing them sensory overload and overwhelm. Intervention is critical for addressing the child's sensory needs.

Sleep patterns

Children with sleeping difficulties or who don't get adequate sleep may be too tired, which can influence their behaviour and make them unwilling to wake up early to go to school. Persistent poor sleep quality or insufficient sleep causes difficulties with attention, memory and reasoning, problem solving and lowers the child's ability to control their emotions and behaviours. Intervention is critical for addressing the child's sleep needs.

Eating and drinking skills

A child could have significant nutrition and energy difficulties if they have a lack of food, are picky eaters or have eating disorders, which will impair their immune system and make the child more vulnerable to illness. Absences from school because of illness or medical appointments causes the child to have difficulty keeping up with the curriculum and thus puts them at risk for SRB (Mogensen & Yiu, 2016). Intervention is critical for addressing the child's eating and/or drinking skills.

Communication skills

Communication is a two-way process involving an exchange and flow of information and ideas between no fewer than two people. Classrooms are communication-rich environments but if the child has difficulty with understanding and expressing themselves they are going to have lots of difficulties. Comprehension difficulties will result in the child having trouble understanding language, completing their schoolwork or participating in classroom discussions. Difficulties with expression will limit the child's ability to communicate their needs, thoughts or wants in a clear, coherent and detailed manner for the listener to fully understand the issue and address it in a timely manner. Consequently, the child will experience repeated frustration, failure and rejection which will affect the child's self-esteem, motivation and willingness to attend school. Intervention is critical for addressing the child's communication skills.

Emotional regulation skills

Emotional regulation is the ability to identify, express and manage emotions in healthy ways. A child may have difficulty with identifying the emotions they are experiencing and expressing what they are feeling in appropriate ways which may result in miscommunication and lead to frustration. The child may not know how to manage their emotions causing them to become overwhelmed by particular feelings, whether positive (e.g. happy, overexcited or proud) or negative (e.g. angry, hungry, tired, frustrated, fearful, stressed or disappointed). Consequently, the brain gets flooded by the emotion, which lowers the brain's ability to think and act rationally. The child needs to have the tools to manage their emotions in a healthy way. Without these skills, the child will feel overwhelmed by particular emotions and this may result in the child engaging in SRB. Intervention is critical for addressing the child's emotional regulation skills.

Social skills

Social skills are the non-verbal and verbal communications skills used to interact with others, according to the social conventions of a particular context. Non-verbal communication skills include body language, facial expressions, posture, proximity, listening, grooming and hygiene. Verbal communication skills include greeting others, gaining attention, asking for help, sharing, turn-taking, conversational skills, group work, problem solving and making friends. Children who have social skills difficulties may struggle with many of these skills.

Extensive research has shown that children who exhibit SRB tend to have poor social skills with peers and/or teachers. (e.g., Place et al, 2002; Gonzálvez, 2019). Children who have social skills difficulties may struggle with, for example, conversational skills, making friends and problem solving. They may therefore deal with conflict by making negative behavioural choices. Poor social skills place the child at risk of social isolation, exclusion, rejection and being victimised (Bukowski & Adams, 2005; Boivin et al. 1995, Gazelle & Ladd 2003). Intervention is critical for addressing the child's social skills.

Learning skills

Learning disability, learning disorder or specific learning disorder is a neurodevelopmental disorder that begins during school-age, affects the acquisition, organisation, retention, understanding or use of specific skills (e.g., reading, writing, and maths), which are the foundation for academic learning. Types of learning disorders include dyslexia (difficulty with reading and spelling), dysgraphia (difficulty with writing) and dyscalculia (difficulty with maths) (APA, 2013).

Learning disabilities result from impairments in one or more cognitive processes related to perceiving, thinking, remembering or learning. These include, but are not limited to, difficulties with language processing, phonological processing, visual spatial processing, processing speed, memory, attention and executive functions (e.g. planning, organising, sequencing and decision making) (British Columbia School Superintendents' Association, 2011).

When children struggle with learning or find it hard to cope with increasing workload, they experience repeated failure, rejection and frustration. This results in the child experiencing mixed emotions, such as embarrassment, inferiority, insecurity, sadness, anger and anxiety. Missing school or classes becomes a vicious cycle because this compounds the frustrations in learning as the child falls further behind in the classroom.

Gifted children are also at risk of exhibiting SRB if teaching arrangements are inadequate, creating a lack of interest, challenge and motivation to attend school. Experiencing these emotions on a regular, ongoing basis can lead to a child exhibiting avoidance behaviour or SRB. Intervention is critical for addressing the child's learning skills.

Problem-solving skills

Problem-solving is defined as the process or act of finding a solution to a problem. Children who have difficulties with generating solutions and evaluating the consequences of their actions make choices that will further compound the problem. Intervention is critical for addressing the child's problem-solving skills.

Interests, likes and dislikes

Knowing the child's interests, likes and dislikes can give insight into what may be triggering the SRB. For example, a child is more likely to come to school when Japanese is on because that's their favourite lesson but less likely to come when English is on. A child is more likely to skip school a few days before the camp, the actual camp and a few days after camp. A child who enjoys playing on the X-box may find it rewarding staying at home playing it all night and thus does not attend school the next day.

Major life events the child has experienced

Have a discussion with the child's parents and caregivers, to discover if there have been changes in the child's family or home situation recently that might affect the child's behaviour (e.g. moving homes, new sibling being born or sibling moving out). In these situations, some children exhibit emotional and behavioural difficulties, but gradually return to their previous functioning over time. However, there are some events that can have severe and long-lasting events, namely traumatic events.

The Diagnostic and Statistical Manual of Mental Disorders 5th edition (DSM-5) [American Psychiatric Publishing (APA), 2013], is a handbook that is used by mental health professionals. The DSM-5 defines trauma as "Exposure to actual or threatened death, serious injury, or sexual violence in one (or more) of the following ways: directly experiencing the traumatic event(s); witnessing, in person, the traumatic event(s) as it occurred to others; learning that the traumatic event(s) occurred to a close family member or close friend (in case of actual or threatened death of a family member or friend, the event(s) must have been violent or accidental); or experiencing repeated or extreme exposure to aversive details of the traumatic event(s)" (APA, 2013, p. 271).

Children vary in their reactions and responses to traumatic events. It is important that children who have experienced one or more traumatic events (e.g. divorce, loss of a loved one and being bullied) receive ongoing support to work through their experiences. Without ongoing support, the stress related to the traumatic event lingers and alters the brain which can have lasting effects on the child's development, growth and functioning. This results in the child having difficulty with learning new skills and regressing by losing previously acquired skills causing changes in the child's cognitive, physical, social, emotional, communication and behavioural skills. Intervention is critical for helping the child develop these skills.

Describe the child's challenging behaviour related to school refusal

With the team, review and discuss the child's school attendance history to write a detailed, objective and specific description of what the challenging behaviour looks like at school. For example, instead of: 'Anh will complain she is sick,' a better description would be, 'In the classroom, Anh will stop doing her work, walk up to the teacher and state she has a stomach ache so needs to go to the sick bay.' The latter description is specific, observable and measurable so that anyone who is not present has a clear picture of it.

Use the *Child's Profile* form provided below to answer the questions as applicable. When answering the questions below describe as much detail as possible.

Child's Profile

Name	Date of birth
Contributor name	Contributor role
Address	Date completed

General health

Visual skills

Hearing skills

Physical skills

Sensory needs

Sleep patterns

Eating and drinking skills

Communication skills

Emotional regulation skills

Social skills

Learning skills

Problem-solving skills

Interests, likes and dislikes

Major life events the child has experienced

Describe the child's challenging behaviours related to school refusal

Other comments

Behaviour Data Collection Forms

The next type of assessment involves measuring the challenging behaviour. This means noting the behaviour's frequency, duration and intensity over the course of at least a few weeks or longer.

Use the Behaviour *Data Collection* form provided on the following page to track and collect the following:

- School attendance - Tick if the child attended school or did not attend school on a particular day.
- Session attendance – On the days the child was at school, then for the sessions the child attended, if the child attended the class/session record the start and finish time they stayed in class.
- Challenging behaviour data – Record measurable details about the challenging behaviour by using the *Frequency* (how often it occurs), *Duration* (how long it can last) and *Intensity* (how severe it is) forms provided on the following pages to collate the data over a course of at least a few weeks or longer.

Behaviour Data Collection Form

Child name _____

Recorder name/s _____

School name _____

Describe the challenging behaviour in specific, observable and measurable terms:

Timetable	Date: _____ ☐ Attended school ☐ Did not attend school
Session 1 Subject:	☐ Attended ☐ Stayed in class from to Use tally marks to record number of times behaviour occurred Rate severity of behaviour Mild Moderate Severe
Session 2 Subject:	☐ Attended ☐ Stayed in class from to Use tally marks to record number of times behaviour occurred Rate severity of behaviour Mild Moderate Severe
Recess	☐ Attended ☐ Stayed in class from to Use tally marks to record number of times behaviour occurred Rate severity of behaviour Mild Moderate Severe
Session 3 Subject:	☐ Attended ☐ Stayed in class from to Use tally marks to record number of times behaviour occurred Rate severity of behaviour Mild Moderate Severe
Session 4 Subject:	☐ Attended ☐ Stayed in class from to Use tally marks to record number of times behaviour occurred Rate severity of behaviour Mild Moderate Severe
Lunch	☐ Attended ☐ Stayed in class from to Use tally marks to record number of times behaviour occurred Rate severity of behaviour Mild Moderate Severe
Session 5 Subject:	☐ Attended ☐ Stayed in class from to Use tally marks to record number of times behaviour occurred Rate severity of behaviour Mild Moderate Severe

Based on the information collected, write a summary identifying any patterns:

- Are there any specific days when the child is most likely to not attend? If yes, record _____

- Are there any specific days when the child is most likely to attend? If yes, record _____

- Are there any specific subjects that the child is most likely to not attend? If yes, record names of subject _____

- Are there any specific subjects that the child is most likely to attend? If yes, record names of subjects _____

- Are there any subjects / sessions where the child does not stay for the entire session? _____

Functional Behaviour Analysis (FBA)

A Functional Behaviour Analysis (FBA) is a systematic and collaborative problem-solving process (Ohio Department of Education, 2002). FBA involves reflecting on an incident when the challenging behaviour occurred to identify what triggered it and the purpose (function) that the behaviour served. It is a process that aims to analyse the antecedents (what preceded the behaviour), the behaviour itself and the consequence (what happened immediately after the behaviour).

FBA → Complete 'Document incident'

To complete the FBA, log on to the Behaviour Help web-based app. The user can systematically analyse a recent incident by completing an FBA in the assessment section of the web-based app. Start by selecting 'document incident'. Alternatively, details can be recorded on paper using the *Antecedent – Behaviour – Consequence* form provided at the end of this section.

The following information shows what to include and how to answer the questions posed by the FBA.

FBA → Complete 'Record incident' details

What?	Record the details of the incident.
Why?	These details will provide insight into the situations where the challenging behaviours related to SRB occur.
How?	Record the information in the web-based app or in the *Antecedent – Behaviour – Consequence* form provided at the end of this section. Date – Record the date the incident occurred. Time started – Record the time the incident started. Ended – Record the time the incident finished. During – Record the activity that was happening at the time of the incident. Where – Record the location of the incident. Who - Record the names of people who were involved in the incident.

FBA → Complete 'Analyse incident'→ Antecedent

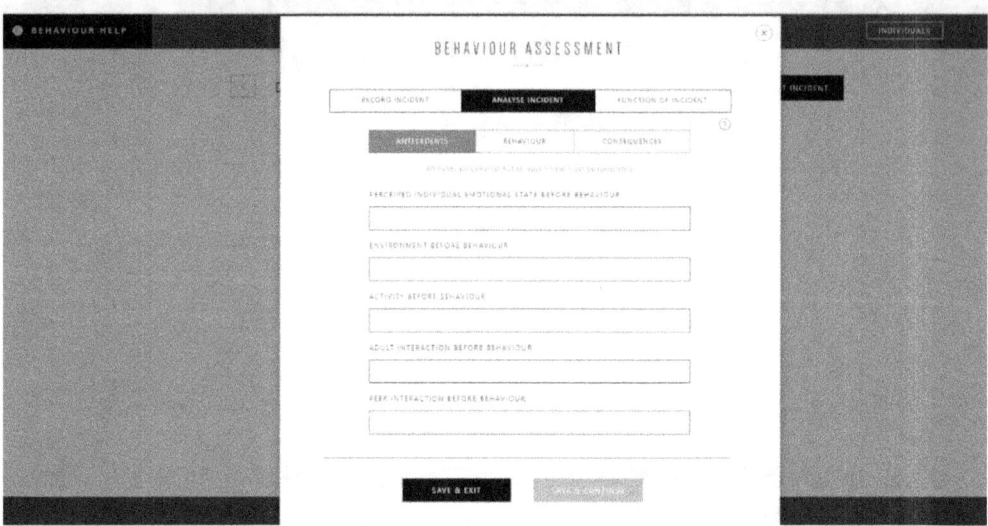

What?	Record the events (antecedents) that immediately preceded the behaviour.
Why?	It is important to identify what may have triggered the child's behaviour. This information can then be used to identify intervention strategies to prevent and manage the behaviour in the future.
How?	The next couple of pages provide a comprehensive list of potential triggers related to the child, interaction, activity or environment that could have contributed to the child's SRB behaviour. With the help of the team, select the options that apply and/or edit the text as appropriate. Record the information in the *Antecedent – Behaviour – Consequence* form provided at the end of this section. Alternatively, select from predefined triggers in the Behaviour Help web-based app and add any of the SRB behaviour-customised triggers shown below.

Antecedent

Perceived child emotional state before challenging behaviour	☐ Angry ☐ Bored ☐ Calm ☐ Frustrated ☐ Happy ☐ Hungry ☐ In pain

	☐ Jealous ☐ Lonely ☐ Overexcited ☐ Overstimulated ☐ Scared ☐ Stressed ☐ Tense ☐ Thirsty ☐ Tired ☐ Uncomfortable ☐ Unsafe ☐ Unwell ☐ Upset ☐ Worried ☐ Other
Environmental context before challenging behaviour	☐ Not applicable <u>General aspects</u> ☐ Non-preferred environment ☐ Transition between environments ☐ Unfamiliar environment <u>Sensory aspects</u> *Tactile (touch) aspects* ☐ Too cold ☐ Too hot *Olfactory (smell) aspects* ☐ Non-preferred odour ☐ Preferred odour ☐ Strong odour *Proprioceptive (body awareness) aspects* ☐ Had insufficient personal space ☐ Too crowded *Auditory aspects* ☐ Too noisy ☐ Too quiet

	Visual aspects ☐ Bright lights ☐ Too dark ☐ Visually cluttered ☐ Visually under stimulating ☐ Other
Peer context before challenging behaviour	☐ Not applicable ☐ Bullied child ☐ Denied child request ☐ Entered room ☐ Gave high levels of attention ☐ Gave low levels of attention ☐ Ignored child ☐ Left room ☐ Moved away ☐ Laughed at child ☐ Reacted to child ☐ Touched child ☐ Touched child's belongings ☐ Other
Adult context before challenging behaviour	☐ Not applicable *Adult present* ☐ Non-preferred adult present ☐ Preferred adult absent ☐ Preferred adult present ☐ Regular adult absent ☐ Unfamiliar adult present *Adult attention* ☐ Gave high levels of attention ☐ Gave low levels of attention ☐ Gave others attention ☐ Ignored child ☐ Moved away ☐ Moved closer ☐ Touched child

	Adult communication ☐ Asked a question suddenly ☐ Asked child to wait ☐ Attacked character ☐ Backed child into a corner ☐ Brought up unrelated events ☐ Denied child request ☐ Gave child corrective feedback ☐ Gave child negative feedback ☐ Gave complex directions ☐ Gave inconsistent directions ☐ Gave unclear directions ☐ Insisted on having the last word ☐ Made unsubstantiated accusations ☐ Mimicked child ☐ Offered assistance without asking ☐ Offered praise ☐ Raised voice ☐ Said 'no', 'not to', 'stop', 'don't' or 'wait' ☐ Used degrading, insulting, humiliating or embarrassing put downs ☐ Used negative tone of voice ☐ Used sarcasm ☐ Used tense body language ☐ Used unwarranted physical force ☐ Other
Activity context before challenging behaviour	☐ Not applicable General aspects ☐ Activity started late ☐ Difficult ☐ Disliked activity that was offered ☐ Easy ☐ Finished early ☐ Lost a game ☐ Failed in the activity ☐ Flow was interrupted ☐ Group work ☐ Incorrect equipment

- [ ] Independent work
- [ ] Information about upcoming activity was not given
- [ ] Insufficient equipment
- [ ] Long
- [ ] Long waiting periods
- [ ] Many decision-making opportunities
- [ ] No decision-making opportunities
- [ ] Preferred activity stopped
- [ ] Repetitive
- [ ] Requested activity denied
- [ ] Transition occurred without sufficient warning
- [ ] Transition was rushed
- [ ] Transitions
- [ ] Unexpected changes
- [ ] Unfamiliar
- [ ] Unstructured

<u>Sensory aspects</u>

Visual aspects
- [ ] Non-preferred visual tasks
- [ ] Preferred visual tasks
- [ ] Small font and size
- [ ] Too much visual information

Tactile (touch) aspects
- [ ] Clothing seemed uncomfortable
- [ ] Disliked the textures of the activity materials
- [ ] Insufficient touch
- [ ] Item involved preferred touch
- [ ] Liked the textures of the activity materials
- [ ] Too much touch
- [ ] Unexpected touch

Auditory (sound) aspects
- [ ] Equipment was too loud
- [ ] Interrupted by sudden loud noises
- [ ] Non-preferred auditory elements
- [ ] Preferred auditory elements
- [ ] Too much auditory information

Proprioceptive (body awareness) aspects
- ☐ Child's body position seemed uncomfortable
- ☐ Child's seating equipment seemed uncomfortable
- ☐ Complex motor planning/control and body awareness tasks
- ☐ Did not provide sufficient heavy work/resistive input
- ☐ Required postural control

Olfactory (smell) aspects
- ☐ Non-preferred odour
- ☐ Preferred odour
- ☐ Strong odour

Gustatory (taste) aspects
- ☐ Engagement with food items
- ☐ Non-preferred taste
- ☐ Preferred non-food items
- ☐ Preferred taste

Vestibular (movement) aspects
- ☐ Did not include movement tasks
- ☐ Non-preferred movement tasks
- ☐ Preferred movement tasks
- ☐ Too many movement tasks
- ☐ Other

FBA → Complete 'Analyse incident' → Behaviour

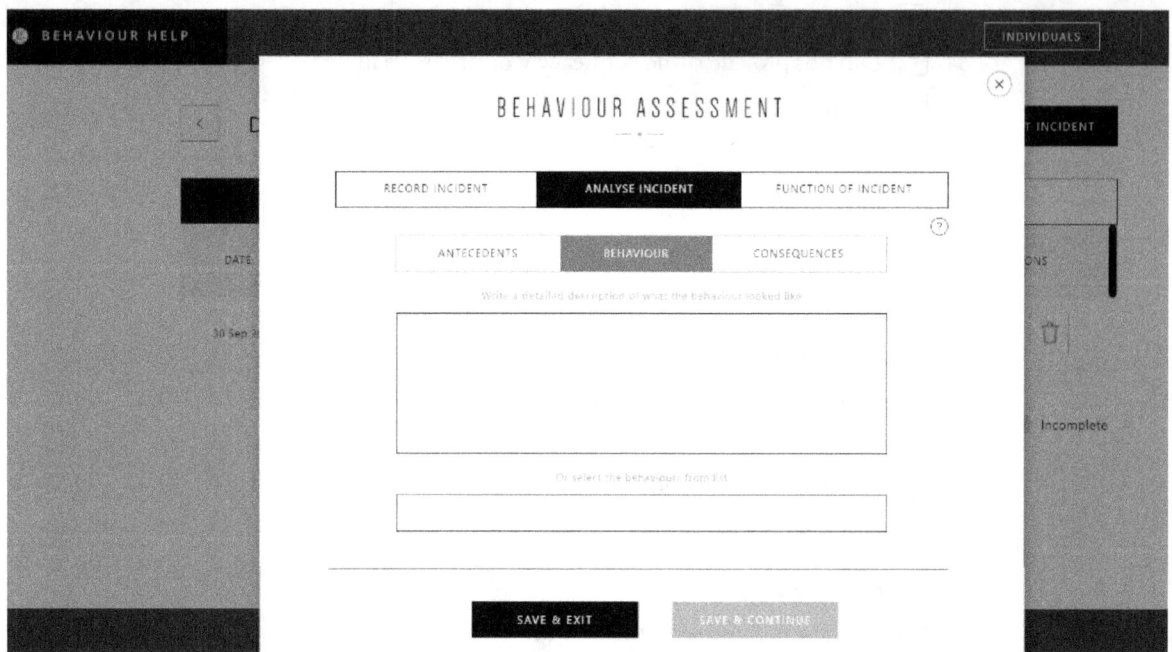

What?	Provide a description of the child's SRB during the incident in observable and measurable terms.
Why?	Describing behaviour in these terms instead of a vague description will allow others who were not present to have a clear picture of what the challenging behaviour looks like.
How?	With the help of the team, write a detailed description that is specific, observable and measurable. For example, "Ten minutes into the English class Anh stopped doing her work, walked up to the teacher and stated she had a stomach ache so needed to go to the sick bay." If recorded on paper, complete the *Antecedent-Behaviour-Consequence* form provided at the end of this section. Alternatively, enter the information in the web-based app.

FBA → Complete 'Analyse incident' → Consequences

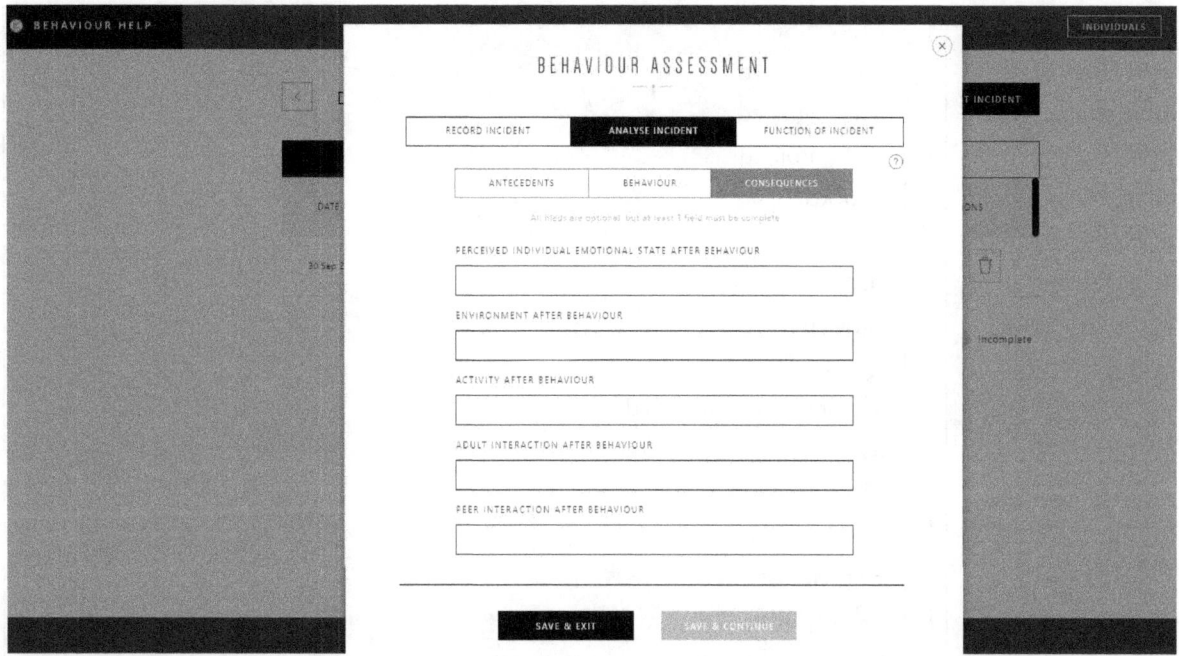

What?	Record the events (consequences) that followed the challenging behaviour.
Why?	This will help identify the events following the SRB that could be strengthening, maintaining or reinforcing it.
How?	As a team, identify which of the subheadings listed on the next few pages relate to the consequence/s of the child's behaviour. Record the information in the *Antecedent – Behaviour – Consequence* form provided at the end of this section. Alternatively, select from predefined triggers in the Behaviour Help web-based app and add any of the SRB behaviour-customised triggers shown below.

Consequences

Perceived child emotional state after challenging behaviour	☐ More upset ☐ More worried ☐ More agitated ☐ More aroused ☐ Shocked ☐ Calm ☐ Better ☐ Satiated ☐ Quieter ☐ Thirst seemed quenched ☐ More comfortable ☐ More tired ☐ Felt safer ☐ Felt relieved ☐ Felt happier ☐ Other
Environmental context after challenging behaviour	☐ Not applicable <u>General aspects</u> ☐ Removed from environment ☐ Returned to preferred environment *Tactile (touch) aspects* ☐ Temperature was increased ☐ Temperature was decreased *Olfactory (smell) aspects* ☐ Moved to an environment with decreased odour ☐ Moved to an environment with preferred odour *Auditory aspects* ☐ Moved to a quieter environment ☐ Moved to a noisier environment *Proprioceptive (body awareness) aspects* ☐ Child offered personal space ☐ Child moved away from others

	Visual aspects ☐ Moved to an environment with dimmer lights ☐ Moved to an environment with brighter lights ☐ Moved to an environment with less clutter ☐ Moved to an environment with more visual stimulation ☐ Other
Peer context after challenging behaviour	☐ Not applicable ☐ Ignored child ☐ Gave higher levels of attention ☐ Gave lower levels of attention ☐ Moved away from the child ☐ Reprimanded for bullying behaviour ☐ Other
Adult context after challenging behaviour	☐ Not applicable ☐ Other familiar adult entered room ☐ Child was removed from the room ☐ Gave child phone to call home ☐ Gave child permission to go home ☐ Guided child to sick bay ☐ Gave low levels of attention ☐ Gave high levels of attention ☐ Gave others attention ☐ Stopped what they were doing ☐ Ignored child ☐ Moved away ☐ Moved closer ☐ Touched child ☐ Preferred adult moved closer ☐ Left child alone ☐ Gave child access to preferred items ☐ Used sarcasm ☐ Used negative tone of voice ☐ Raised voice ☐ Used unwarranted physical force ☐ Left child alone ☐ Talked ☐ Gave clearer directions

	☐ Gave simpler directions ☐ Gave requested item ☐ Other
Activity context after challenging behaviour	☐ Not applicable General aspects ☐ Easier activity was offered ☐ Correct equipment was offered ☐ Preferred activity continued ☐ Preferred activity was offered ☐ Child left alone to work by themselves ☐ Requested activity was provided ☐ Activity was ceased ☐ Child was removed from activity ☐ Child was offered choice of other activities ☐ Non-preferred activity was discontinued Sensory aspects *Olfactory (smell) aspects* ☐ Item with non-preferred odour removed ☐ Item with a preferred odour offered *Visual aspects* ☐ Offered preferred visual tasks ☐ Offered an activity with reduced visual content *Auditory (sound) aspects* ☐ Loud equipment was removed ☐ Moved away from loud equipment ☐ Offered preferred auditory items ☐ Auditory information in activity reduced ☐ Preferred auditory items offered ☐ Non-preferred auditory items removed *Gustatory (taste) aspects* ☐ Items with non-preferred taste removed ☐ Items with preferred taste offered ☐ Preferred non-edible items consumed ☐ Activity with food items removed

Vestibular (movement) aspects
- ☐ Movement tasks offered
- ☐ Movement tasks ceased
- ☐ Movement tasks reduced

Tactile (touch) aspects
- ☐ Deep pressure touch offered
- ☐ Light pressure touch offered
- ☐ Comfortable clothing offered
- ☐ Body position changed
- ☐ Uncomfortable clothing removed
- ☐ Items with preferred touch offered
- ☐ Different seating equipment offered
- ☐ Items with non-preferred touch removed
- ☐ Other

FBA → Complete 'Analyse incident' → Incident function

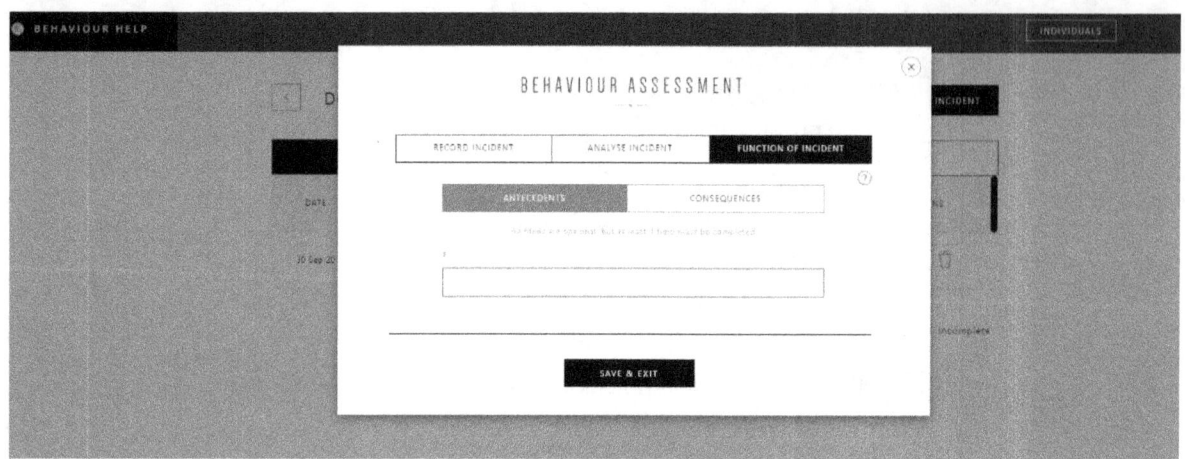

What?	Reflect on the antecedents (what preceded the behaviour) and consequences (what happened immediately after the behaviour) to determine the function/s (purpose) of the challenging behaviour related to school refusal and create a hypothesis.
Why?	By understanding the purpose of the behaviour, the antecedents or the consequences can be addressed to prevent recurrence of the behaviour. The child can also be taught the appropriate alternative behaviour they can use to achieve the purpose instead of the challenging behaviours related to school refusal.
How?	It is important to remember that the one behaviour may serve different functions at different times. As a team, identify which of the subheadings listed and/or in the Behaviour Help web-based app hypothesise the function/s of the behaviour. Review the following descriptions to identify what are the function/s of the challenging behaviours related to school refusal. For example, during science class, Anh will put her head down to escape/avoid doing the assigned work. If recorded on paper, complete the *Antecedent-Behaviour-Consequence* form provided at the end of this section. Alternatively, select from predefined functions in the Behaviour Help web-based app and add any of the behaviour-customised functions shown below.

Incident functions

Function	The child engages in the challenging behaviours to:
Tangible	☐ Get/obtain an object or participate in an activity
Attention	☐ Get/obtain positive or negative social attention or interaction from another.
Sensory input or stimulation	☐ Get/obtain some form of sensory input or stimulation (i.e. visual, auditory, olfactory, gustatory, tactile, vestibular or proprioceptive).
Power/influence/ control	☐ Get/obtain power to cause, direct or prevent actions/reactions/events.
Status	☐ Get/obtain a rank or position.
Revenge	☐ Get/obtain revenge for the perceived or real hurt or harm caused by someone else.
Escape	☐ Avoid/get away from receiving an object or participating in an activity. ☐ Avoid/get away from positive or negative social attention or interaction from an another. ☐ Avoid/get away from receiving some form of sensory input or stimulation. ☐ Avoid/get away from having the ability to make or prevent actions/reactions/events from happening. ☐ Avoid/get away from obtaining a rank or position.

Antecedent-Behaviour-Consequence Form

Child name _____ Date _____

Recorder name/s _____

During (Activity happening at the time of incident) _____

Time started _____ Time ended _____

Where (Location of incident) _____

Who (people involved in incident) _____

	Antecedent	Behaviour	Consequence	Hypothesised Function
Perceived individual state				
Environment				
Activity				
Adult interaction				
Peer interaction				

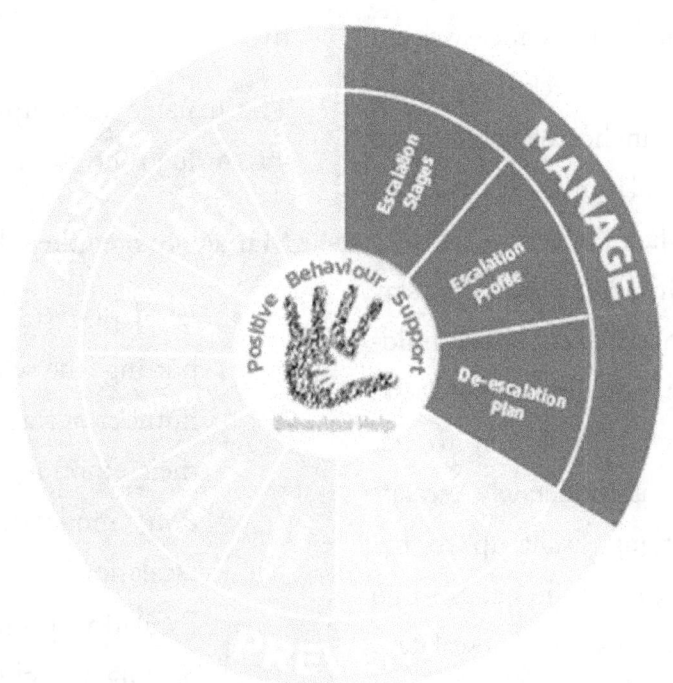

6. MANAGE STAGE

SRB is the result of a complex combination of factors so a team approach that includes the caregivers, school, professionals and other community agencies is required to address SRB.

In this guide the focus is on what the school can do within its context to support the child and the team with the aim of increasing the probability of helping the child to consistently attend and remain at school.

The Manage stage recognises when the child attends school despite all the support and strategies, there will be times when the child will be triggered and experience negative emotions (e.g. anxiety, stress and frustration). Without early and effective management, the child's emotions and behaviours will escalate (rise and become more serious).

For example, Anh has returned to school after being away for two terms. The first couple of weeks she attended school for one period in a week and that went smoothly. After three weeks Anh's attendance was increased to two lessons in a week. Her teachers noticed a change in her behaviour and she has had a few escalations. Her teachers have reported that when Anh is in the calm stage, she will talk in a normal voice, stay seated and do her work. When Anh is mildly escalated, she will stop doing her work, put her head down and hold on to her stomach. When Anh is moderately escalated, she will start crying, walk up to the teacher and tell the teacher she needs to go to the sick bay. If she is extremely escalated, she will then start swearing, screaming and throwing whatever she can around the room. After twenty minutes she will enter the recovery stage by crying, apologising and calm down. Her teachers are unsure what to do as they do not want to make the situation worse, cause setbacks in Anh's progress and contribute to the recurrence of the SRB.

The manage stage of PBS involves recognising the behaviours related to the stages of escalation, identifying effective responses and strategies to safely defuse, redirect and de-escalate the situation in the least disruptive manner.

The manage stage involves the team working through the checklist tasks listed:

Manage Stage Checklist:

- Escalation stages – Help those supporting the child to recognise the number of stages the child exhibits as their emotion rises (i.e. mild escalation, moderate escalation, extreme escalation and recovery stage).
- Escalation profile – Help those supporting the child to recognise what the non-verbal and/or verbal behaviours exhibit in the different escalation stages and how long it can last.
- De-escalation plan – Help those supporting the child with guidelines on how to immediately respond when the behaviour occurs, safely defuse and de-escalate the situation in the least disruptive manner.

Escalation Stages

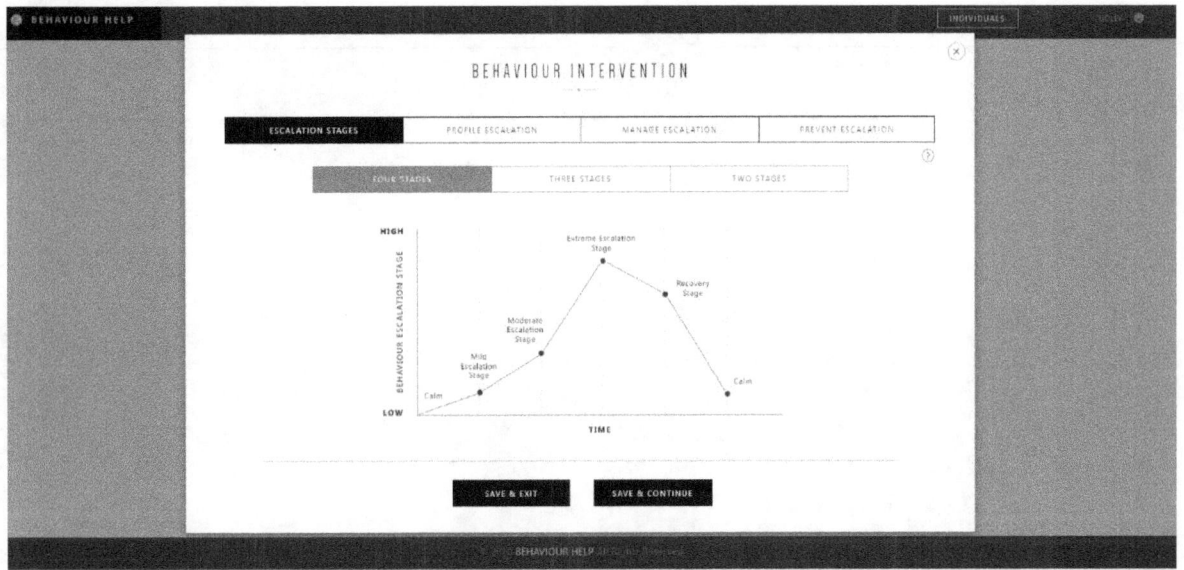

As a child's level of emotion intensity (strength) increases, the behaviour escalates.

This escalation can be seen in stages:

- Calm stage - the child is relatively calm, composed and cooperative.
- Mild escalation stage - the child becomes increasingly unfocused, upset and stressed.
- Moderate escalation stage - the child is non-compliant, confrontational and less logical.
- Extreme escalation stage- the child is out of control, irrational and needs to rage it out.
- Recovery stage - the child calms down and is willing to participate in activities.

Each child is unique and experiences the escalation stages differently. The child may go through all four stages or only some stages. Chart the escalation stages for the child by identifying and selecting the number of stages the child experiences (e.g. five, four, three or two stages) in the Behaviour Help web-based app. Alternatively, the observed stages can be marked on the *Escalation Stages* form below.

Escalation Stages Form

Child name _____ Date _____

Recorder name/s _____

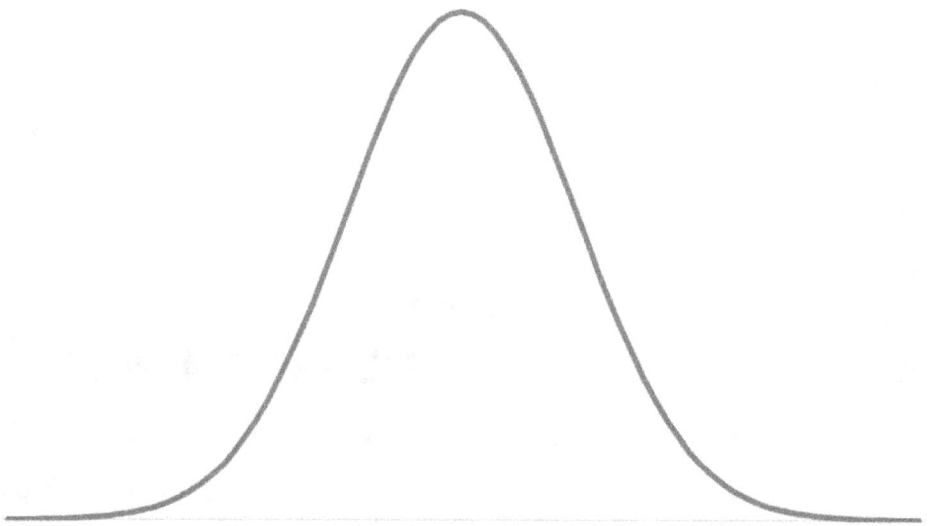

Escalation Profile

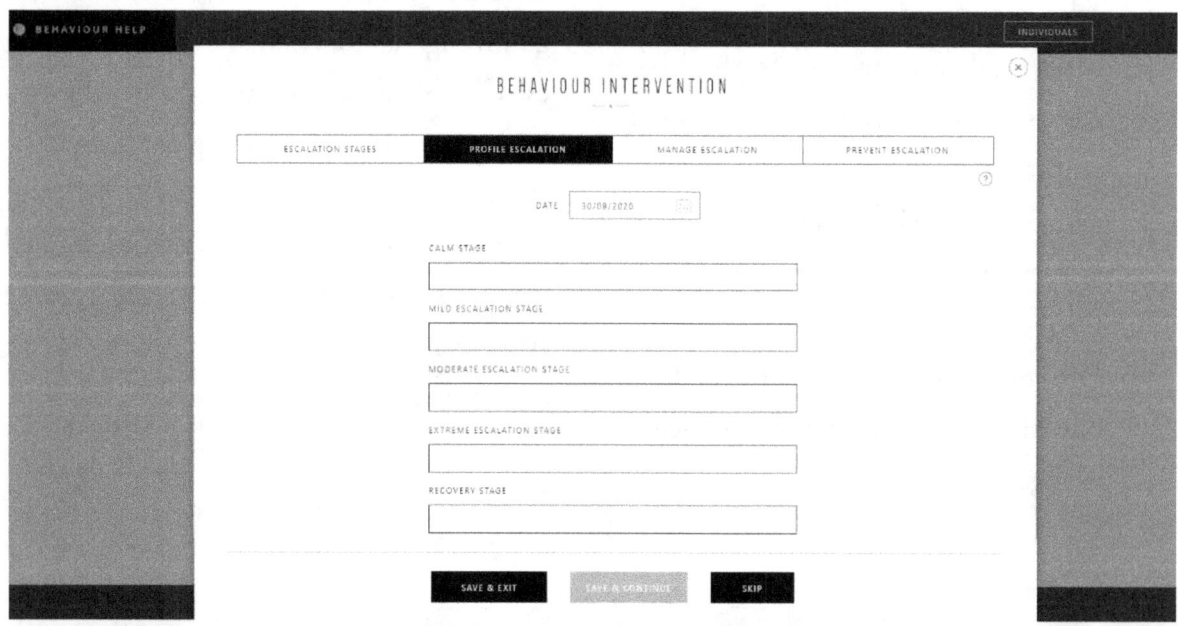

Once the number of escalation stages the child experiences has been charted, the next step is to identify the non-verbal and/or verbal behaviours the child exhibits in each stage. The child may exhibit behaviours that are directed towards the external environment and/or behaviours that are directed towards the self in the different stages of escalation.

The child will exhibit a range of behaviours in the different stages of escalation. For example, a child will go from a calm stage (e.g. quiet voice, staying seated and listening) to mild escalation (e.g. loud voice, throwing a book on the floor and standing in a defensive posture with arms crossed) to moderate escalation (e.g. swearing, pacing and clenched fists) to extreme escalation (e.g. hitting, kicking and screaming) and finally the recovery stage (e.g. crying, apologising and calming down).

Develop an escalation profile plan with the team, by identifying and selecting externalised and internalised behaviours the child exhibits in each stage. Externalised challenging behaviours are those that are directed towards the external environment and/or internalised challenging behaviours are those that are directed towards the self.

To help the team recognise the behaviours the child exhibits in each escalation stage please refer to the list provided on the following pages and/or click on 'Or select the behaviours from the escalation stage list' in the web-based app.

Externalised challenging behaviours

Aggressive behaviour	Verbally aggressive behaviours
	☐ Attempting to draw people into a power struggle
	☐ Attempting to draw people into an argument
	☐ Interrupting others
	☐ Provoking a confrontation
	☐ Screaming at others
	☐ Swearing at others
	☐ Threatening others
	☐ Yelling out inappropriate comments
	Physically aggressive behaviours
	☐ Biting
	☐ Choking

	☐ Hitting ☐ Kicking ☐ Pinching ☐ Pulling hair ☐ Punching ☐ Pushing ☐ Scratching ☐ Stealing ☐ Tripping ☐ Other	
Disorganised behaviour	☐ Compulsive ☐ Dropping to the floor ☐ Frantic ☐ Overactive ☐ Pausing between actions ☐ Restless ☐ Running away ☐ Other	
Disruptive behaviour	☐ Bragging ☐ Chronic blurting out ☐ Clowning around ☐ Copying another's speech ☐ Frequently making noises ☐ Hand raising all the time ☐ Inappropriate sexual behaviour ☐ Laughing inappropriately ☐ Lying ☐ Making prejudicial remarks: ○ Religious ○ Sexual orientation ○ Racial ☐ Needing someone to help, teach or watch them do something ☐ Repeatedly seeking validation ☐ Spreading rumours ☐ Talking excessively ☐ Tattling ☐ Teasing ☐ Telling fantastical stories	

	☐ Using a loud and animated voice ☐ Other	
Self-injurious behaviour	☐ Banging ☐ Biting ☐ Burning ☐ Cutting ☐ Ingesting dangerous substance ☐ Inhaling dangerous substance ☐ Overdosing on medication ☐ Picking ☐ Poking ☐ Refusing food ☐ Refusing medication ☐ Scratching ☐ Slapping ☐ Twisting ☐ Other	
Destructive behaviour	☐ Breaking ☐ Burning ☐ Damaging ☐ Graffitiing ☐ Overturning ☐ Picking ☐ Pulling apart ☐ Smashing ☐ Stealing ☐ Tearing ☐ Throwing ☐ Other	
Self-stimulatory behaviour	<u>Proprioceptive</u> ☐ Biting self ☐ Chewing on things ☐ Crashing into people ☐ Crashing into things ☐ Grinding teeth ☐ Slamming things	

Gustatory
- ☐ Eating non-food items
- ☐ Licking objects
- ☐ Mouthing objects
- ☐ Placing body part in mouth
- ☐ Placing object in mouth
- ☐ Regurgitating
- ☐ Ruminating

Olfactory
- ☐ Holding nose
- ☐ Smelling objects
- ☐ Sniffing people

Vestibular
- ☐ Swinging
- ☐ Tapping foot
- ☐ Flapping hands
- ☐ Spinning
- ☐ Pacing
- ☐ Bouncing
- ☐ Rocking front to back
- ☐ Rocking side to side

Auditory
- ☐ Repetitive questioning
- ☐ Giggling inappropriately
- ☐ Grunting or high-pitched shrieking
- ☐ Repeating phrases, movies quotes, song lyrics, etc.
- ☐ Making loud and/or high-pitched noises
- ☐ Making vocal sounds
- ☐ Banging objects
- ☐ Snapping fingers
- ☐ Tapping ears or objects
- ☐ Humming
- ☐ Covering ears

Visual
- ☐ Flicking fingers

- [ ] Lining things up
- [ ] Looking sideways at things
- [ ] Flapping hands
- [ ] Staring at lights or objects
- [ ] Repetitively blinking
- [ ] Turning on and off light switches
- [ ] Shaking things
- [ ] Throwing or dropping objects
- [ ] Doing a task repetitively
- [ ] Wiggling fingers in front or at side of face
- [ ] Tilting head while watching objects
- [ ] Watching moving objects
- [ ] Waving fingers in front or at side of face
- [ ] Opening and shutting objects
- [ ] Stacking and knocking things down
- [ ] Pacing
- [ ] Spinning things
- [ ] Twirling objects
- [ ] Twirling self
- [ ] Spinning self
- [ ] Walking in patterns
- [ ] Excessive drawing
- [ ] Watching same video repeatedly

<u>Tactile</u>
- [ ] Banging head
- [ ] Biting fingernails
- [ ] Biting self
- [ ] Chewing fingernails
- [ ] Chewing on insides of cheeks
- [ ] Chewing skin
- [ ] Clapping hands
- [ ] Grabbing someone's arm with both hands
- [ ] Grinding teeth
- [ ] Masturbating
- [ ] Mouthing objects
- [ ] Picking skin

- ☐ Pinching self
- ☐ Rubbing clothing between fingers
- ☐ Rubbing face
- ☐ Rubbing hands
- ☐ Rubbing skin
- ☐ Rubbing skin with object
- ☐ Scratching skin
- ☐ Spitting
- ☐ Squeezing head against arm
- ☐ Tapping body part
- ☐ Tapping object
- ☐ Wringing hands
- ☐ Other

Internalised challenging behaviours

- ☐ Appearing excessively shy
- ☐ Appearing sad most of the time
- ☐ Avoiding tasks
- ☐ Avoiding interactions
- ☐ Being indecisive
- ☐ Being excessively timid
- ☐ Being non-responsive
- ☐ Being reluctant to participate
- ☐ Being tearful
- ☐ Engaging in socially isolating behaviours
- ☐ Frequent complaints of pain such as stomach aches, headaches, dizziness or chest pain or illness
- ☐ Hiding behind furniture
- ☐ Hiding under furniture
- ☐ Repeated pleas to call home or go home
- ☐ Seeming excessively embarrassed
- ☐ Seeming excessively fearful
- ☐ Seeming excessively worried
- ☐ Withdrawn
- ☐ Other

Alternatively, details can be recorded on paper using the *Escalation Profile* form provided on the next page.

Escalation Profile Form

Child name _____ Date _____

Recorder name/s _____

Calm Stage
Mild Escalation Stage
Moderate Escalation Stage
Extreme Escalation Stage
Recovery Stage

De-escalation Plan

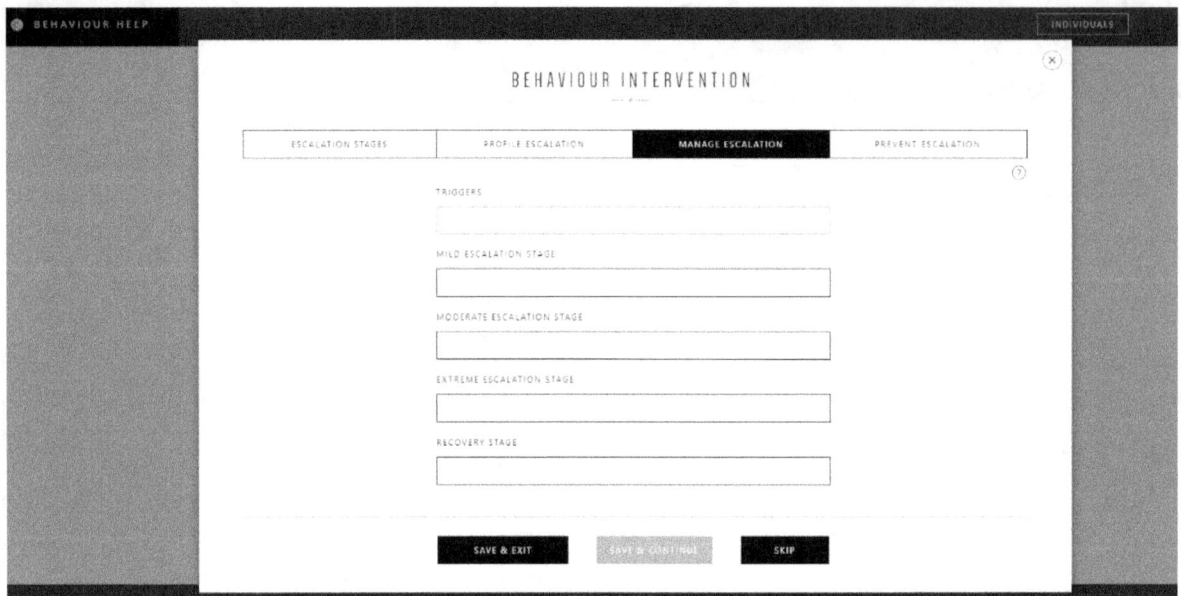

Develop a plan that the team can use to immediately respond to when the child exhibits the challenging behaviour.

The strategies to manage the challenging behaviour are summarised by the acronym **DE-ESCALATION**:

Display calm demeanour
Engage attention
Encourage cooperation
Space to calm
Comfort, support and reassure
Ask what happened
Listen actively and attentively
Acknowledge and validate
Talk about positive attitudes, choices and behaviours
Identify appropriate alternate behaviour
Offer help
Note positives

The explanations for the DE-ESCALATION strategies are provided. Discuss them with the team, select and edit the strategies as appropriate. Not all strategies will suit or meet the child's needs, so select and tailor them based on the advice from the team. If recorded on paper, complete the *De-escalation plan* form provided at the end of this section. In the app, the headings 'Triggers', 'Mild escalation stage', 'Moderate escalation stage', 'Extreme escalation stage' and 'Recovery stage' are used. With the team, firstly record the triggers for the behaviour. Secondly, depending on the number of escalation stages the child exhibits and the range of challenging behaviours the child exhibits, work as a team to identify stage-specific de-escalation strategies. This will enable everyone to take charge of the situation by safely bringing it under control and avoid further escalation of the child's behaviour in consistent ways.

DE-ESCALATION plan → **Display calm demeanour**

What?	Project calm, relaxed and positive body language as you discreetly observe the child.
Why?	Staying calm allows one to think clearly and make better decisions and responses. A calm composure also helps to transfer a sense of calm onto the child.
How?	☐ Take deep breaths. ☐ Appear calm. ☐ Maintain a relaxed facial expression. ☐ Start by strategically ignoring non-threatening and low-level behaviour when it starts. ☐ Ignore the behaviour non-verbally (e.g. do not look, give subtle glances, smile or frown) and verbally (e.g. do not talk to the child) for up to 90 seconds and/or move away from the child for up to 90 seconds to see if the behaviour disappears. ☐ Remind peers of the rules. ☐ If the behaviour does not stop approach progress to 'Engage attention, Encourage cooperation'.

DE-ESCALATION plan → **Engage attention, Encourage cooperation**

What?	Communicate using short, simple and clear speech in a respectful, non-threatening and assertive manner in private to gain the child's attention and cooperation.
Why?	Talking out loud in front of others about what is causing the upset can add to the child's distress make them more self-conscious, raise their anxiety and make them more unwilling to talk. By using a quiet voice and/or talking to the child 1:1 issues can be privately resolved without causing the child embarrassment.
How?	☐ Get close to the child while maintaining a safe distance so that they can see and hear you. ☐ Lower the volume and pitch of your voice. ☐ Ask if the child would like help with the activity. ☐ If the child accepts offer, acknowledge and provide assistance. ☐ If the child does not accept offer, acknowledge and move away for a specific period of time as agreed upon by the team (e.g. one minute or five minutes or ten minutes). ☐ If the behaviour stops, purposefully look for the child's positive behaviours and provide praise. ☐ If the behaviour continues, make eye contact with the child to indicate awareness of behaviour. ☐ Use non-verbal cues or signals to remind the child to stop the behaviour. ☐ If the behaviour stops, purposefully look for the child's positive behaviours and provide praise. ☐ If the behaviour continues, move closer to the child, quietly remind them of what you want them to do and say 'thank you' or 'thanks' at end of the rule. ☐ Move away for a specific period of time as agreed upon by the team (e.g. three minutes or ten minutes) to give the child space to process and decide to comply with instruction. ☐ If the behaviour stops, purposefully look for the child's positive behaviours and provide praise. ☐ If the behaviour continues, alter the level of difficulty, length, time provided, outcome, level of participation, content, materials and sensory input to meet sensory needs. ☐ If the behaviour stops, purposefully look for the child's positive behaviours and provide praise.

	☐ If the behaviour continues, redirect their attention to another topic of conversation or activity, ask child to help or interact with another child or adult, request them to run an errand or move to a different environment.
	☐ If the child complies, purposefully look for the child's positive behaviours and provide praise.
	☐ If the behaviour continues move to 'Space to Calm' strategy.

DE-ESCALATION plan → **Space to calm**

What?	Give the child space and time to calm down.
Why?	To ensure the safety and well-being of the child and everyone around the child it is important to give everyone space. By providing space it allows the child to recover, regain composure and regain control over their emotions and behaviour.
How?	☐ Encourage peers to minimise interaction with the child.
	☐ Encourage other adult/s to minimise interaction with the child.
	☐ Make time immediately to support the child.
	☐ Direct the child to stop routine activity.
	☐ Direct the child to the designated calm down, chill out or sensory area.
	☐ If it is difficult to support and/or supervise the child immediately, accompany the child to a supervised environment (e.g. school counsellor, school psychologist or administration office).
	☐ Alternatively, provide the child with space by sending others away from the area.
	☐ Remove potentially harmful objects.
	☐ Maintain a reasonable distance from the child (left alone or needs adult present in space).
	☐ Allow the child time to rage it out.
	☐ Position yourself closer to the room entrance so you can make a quick exit if required.
	☐ Minimise sudden body movements such as gestures, pacing and fidgeting.
	☐ Place hands in front of the body in an open and relaxed position.
	☐ Give no or minimal eye contact.
	☐ Do not take behaviours personally by remembering it's about the child's own upset and skills gap.
	☐ Do not stand in front facing the child.
	☐ Do not turn your back to the child.
	☐ Do not pace, fidget or shift your weight.

	☐ Do not allow the child to block your exit from the room.
	☐ Do not cross arms, place hands on hips, hands in pockets or arms behind back.
	☐ Do not point or shake your finger at the child.
	☐ Do not use aggressive facial expressions or smile
	☐ Engage in minimal or no talking.
	☐ Ensure that if instructions have to be given, they are kept short and simple.
	☐ State the instruction as a positive (do statement) rather than a negative (don't statement).
	☐ Speak slowly in a calm, low and monotonous voice.
	☐ Ignore and disregard the child's inappropriate language
	☐ Do not raise your voice, yell or scream at the child.
	☐ Do not argue, judge, interrupt or deny what the child says.
	☐ Do not insult, criticise or shame the child.
	☐ Do not discipline.
	☐ Allow the child time to recover.
	☐ Be aware that recovery can take up to 45 minutes or longer.

DE-ES**C**ALATION plan → **Comfort, support and reassurance**

What?	Offer comfort, support and reassurance to the child.
Why?	The best way to support children during their times of distress is by allowing them to express their feelings. By being present the adult can gently guide the child to work through their emotions in healthy ways. Supporting the child in ways that is accepting of their experience and emotion will allow the child to trust, feel safe and strengthen the relationship. This will provide the platform for the child to pay attention to what the adult is saying and cooperate with their suggestions.
How?	☐ Stand side by side or sit side by side when talking to the child to be less confrontational. ☐ Avoid making sustained eye contact (more than 2-3 seconds at a time). ☐ Make eye contact from time to time. ☐ Lower the volume and pitch of voice. ☐ Keep tone even and firm. ☐ Speak at a slower pace. ☐ Respectfully and calmly let the child know you are there to listen, support and assist them in all situations (positive and negative). ☐ Connect by considering the underlying emotion behind the child's behaviour

	based on how they are currently experiencing things from their point of view. For example, 'I can see you are feeling _____'.
	☐ Actively listen to the child.
	☐ Paraphrase by repeating the message back to your child so that you can show that you listened and check that you understood. For example, 'You feel like nobody is listening to you', or 'You are feeling annoyed because _____'.
	☐ Explain to the child that it is important to calm down before talking and sorting through whatever is concerning them.
	☐ Ask the child if they would like to do something that would make them feel better.
	☐ Ask the child if they would like to use relaxation strategies (e.g. deep breathing, counting from 1 to 10, drink of water, mindfulness exercises or listening to soothing music) to calm down.
	☐ Ask the child if they would like sensory activities to help them calm down.
	☐ Ask the child if they would like to go for a walk.
	☐ Use humour to lighten the mood.

DE-ESC**AL**ATION plan → **Ask what happened, Listen actively and attentively**

What?	Ask the child to explain what happened from their perspective.
Why?	To provide support that is sensitive and responsive to the child's needs it is important to tune into and view the situation from their perspective. Listening to the child attentively and fully is essential to relationship building.
How?	☐ Wait for the child to fully recover.
	☐ Talk about the behaviours you have observed.
	☐ Use a neutral and objective statement to enquire about the child's needs and concerns (e.g. 'Please tell me what is going on?', 'Can you tell me what is making you feel ___?' or 'Can you help me understand what happened?' or 'I wonder what caused you ___').
	☐ Listen to both verbal and non-verbal communication with openness to understand what the child is going through.
	☐ Paraphrase by repeating the message back to the child to check they have been understood.
	☐ Do not insult, criticise or shame the child by making remarks that are patronising/belittling/dismissive (e.g. 'Don't worry' 'Calm down', 'Turn that frown up-

	side down', 'You shouldn't feel that way', 'Nobody else feels like that' or 'It'll be okay).
	☐ Clarify by asking open ended questions to get the complete picture of their concerns.
	☐ Do not argue, judge, interrupt or deny what the child says.
	☐ Do not raise voice, yell or scream at the child.

DE-ESCALATION plan → **Acknowledge and validate**

What?	Acknowledge and validate the child's emotions and thoughts.
Why?	Acknowledging and validating the child's emotions and thoughts makes them feel visible, heard and that they are important.
How?	☐ Use empathetic phrases that validate and acknowledge the child's feelings (e.g. 'I can see that you are feeling…', 'I can hear how upset you are…' and 'I am so sorry that happened…'). ☐ Reinforce that it is OK to experience the feelings and emotions but there are OK and not OK ways of expressing them. ☐ Apologise for something you did wrong or the way it was taken (e.g. 'I'm sorry that when I ……. it made you feel …….' and 'That was not my intention…..'). ☐ Thank the child for sharing their concerns, perspectives and difficulties.

DE-ESCALATION plan → **Talk about positive attitudes, choices and behaviours**

What?	Children need to develop positive attitudes, choices and behaviours.
Why?	Children need to develop positive attitudes, choices and behaviours to cope with frustration caused by inconveniences, stressors and problems that stand in the way of their goals.
How?	☐ Remind the child of your helping role. ☐ Discuss how frustrations provide an opportunity for us to grow by helping us develop positive attitudes, make better choices and learn appropriate ways of behaving.

DE-ESCALATION plan → **Identify appropriate alternative behaviour; Offer help; Note positives**

What?	Help the child to reflect on the incident, learn appropriate alternative ways of dealing with similar situations and make amends to repair the relationship.
Why?	It is important to help the child understand the impact of their behaviour on themselves and others. By problem-solving together, it makes the process of talking about the incident less threatening.
How?	☐ Reinforce that you want the best outcome for the child. ☐ Encourage the child to reflect on what went well, what did not work well, and what behaviours need replacing. ☐ Ask the child for ideas on resolving the situation and moving forward. ☐ Listen to their suggestions. ☐ Clarify and repeat the suggestions to the child. ☐ Discuss the consequences of each possible suggestion with the child. ☐ Offer suggestions of possible solutions to the current problem. ☐ Choose the most effective solution i.e. appropriate alternative behaviour collaboratively. ☐ Thank the child for talking through the problem. ☐ Remind the child that they can come and talk anytime. ☐ Set up a regular time to catch up with the child so that their progress can be monitored and any issues or concerns can be addressed in a timely manner. ☐ Help the child to return to previous activity or move on to another activity.

De-escalation Plan Form

Child name _____ Date _____

Recorder name/s _____

Triggers

Mild Escalation Stage

Moderate Escalation Stage

Extreme Escalation Stage

Recovery Stage

7. PREVENT STAGE

SRB occurs when the demands, stress and expectations exceed the child's skills and available supports.

Prevent Stage Checklist:

The Prevent stage involves the team working through the checklist tasks:

- Prevent plan steps - the aim is to first outline the steps that could be taken to gradually progress the child's school attendance from one lesson a week….. few lessons a week …part-time …..full-time on an ongoing basis.

- Prevent plan strategies – the aim is to detail the strategies that should be utilised in each step to minimise or avoid the triggers to maximise the child's success when they are at school. Strategies should be included for how to provide the child with supportive environments, activities and interactions, while making opportunities to teach skills to help them positively behave and manage their emotions.

Discuss the information provided on the following pages with the team. Not all the strategies will suit every context or meet the child's particular needs, so select and tailor them based on the advice from the team as appropriate

Prevent plan steps

To create a plan for successful re-entry to school, use the gradual exposure approach. This approach can be understood by using the analogy of a staircase, where the child begins on the bottom step and the goal is at the top. Each step represents a target that the team would like the child to achieve before moving on to the next step. Each step helps the child progress to attending school for an increased length of time, increased number of classes, increased days and so on.

There is no formula defining what the initial step or following steps should be. Every child's staircase will be unique depending on their circumstance. Based on the collective knowledge the team has of the child, they may be able to identify what each step looks like or define the steps one at a time based on the child's response at each step. The plan will aim to provide a positive experience to the child when they return to school after a period of absence.

Based on the collective knowledge of the team develop the staircase. If possible, ask the child to contribute to the development of the staircase by offering the child a choice to give them a sense of control without overwhelming them. For example, "Would you like to start with one subject per day or 2 subjects per day?".

The first step in the staircase should be a target close to the child's current level of participation and one that they will be able to achieve successfully. A first step might be getting into the car and driving by school, walking to school and walking back home, choosing one subject that the child would like to attend once a week or choosing one subject that the child would like to attend three times a week.

Step 1: For the first 3 days of the first week of school holidays, walk to school and back with a parent or therapist.

Step 2: For the remaining 4 days of the first week of school holidays, walk to school with a parent or therapist, enter the gate and walk home.

Step 3: For the first 3 days of the second week of school holidays, walk to school with a parent or therapist, walk to the music classroom and walk home.

Step 4: For the remaining 4 days of the second week of school holidays, walk to school with a parent or therapist, walk to the music classroom, walk to the administration building, then walk home.

Step 5: When school resumes, attend music class once a week for 3 weeks with observer participation.

Step 6: Attend music class twice a week for 3 weeks with observer participation.

Example staircase for returning to school after missing a full term, based on *John's case study*

Record this information in the *Prevent plan* form provided at the end of this section.

Prevent plan strategies

To help the child be successful in each step it is important to determine the strategies and skills the child needs to perform the step and to arrange any necessary training.

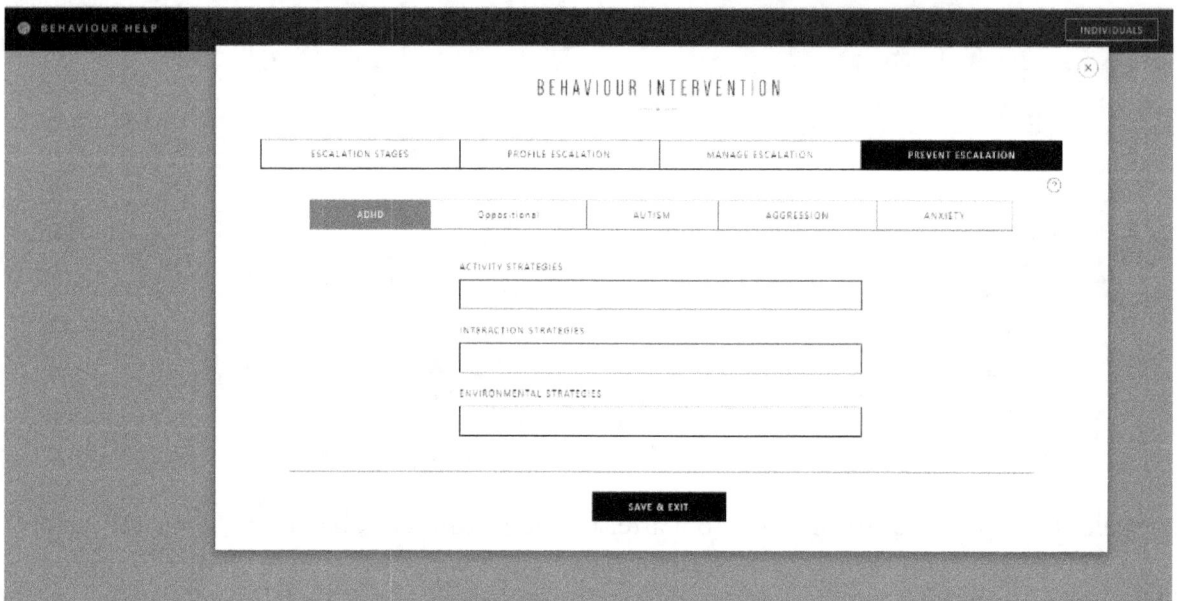

To develop the prevention plan for the child, discuss the strategies listed on the following pages with the team. Not all the strategies will suit every context or meet the child's particular needs, so select and edit them as appropriate. If recorded on paper, complete the *Prevent plan* form provided at the end of this section. Alternatively, if using the Behaviour Help web-based app, start by selecting 'Prevent Escalation' and select the relevant items. Additionally, refer to the following behaviour-customised checklists and add selected items to the app.

It is important the plan is understood by all school staff in order to consistently support the child. Establish a pattern of regular communication with the family to keep them updated with the child's progress with the plan. For example, once a week or more often initially and then every few weeks and longer based on the child's behaviour. Also, remember that some children 'mask' their emotions at school and then release their pent-up emotions at home, so the regular chats can also give insight into how the child is coping with school. If the child is not coping at home discuss with the team if demands in the school context need to be reviewed (e.g. fewer classes, less participation) or progression to the next step be postponed by remaining at the same step for longer in the re-entry plan and not increasing any demands.

Supportive activities → Activity participation

What?	Maintain flexible expectations of the child's level of participation and engagement from activity to activity based on their needs.
Why?	Activity participation demands need to be adjusted to match the child's emotional needs otherwise the child may exhibit challenging behaviours related to school refusal for a variety of functions (e.g. escape/avoid activity and/or gain/obtain adult interaction). As the child gains a sense of control, competence and connection with the activity, the child's level of participation can be gradually increased.

How?	☐ Offer a choice of subjects the child would like to participate in.
	☐ Foster the perspective that success is not defined by the outcome but giving things a go by participating at any level.
	☐ Be responsive to the child's emotional needs by being flexible in participation level expectations.
	☐ Select the level of participation in activities that they are finding challenging by targeting the level closest to where the child is at and can do quite successfully.
	    o Level 1 – Child engages in observer participation by not actively partaking in activity (e.g. not being asked any questions, not required to do any homework, assignments or tests).
	    o Level 2 – Child engages in partial participation by actively partaking in one or more steps/tasks within the activity (e.g. being asked 1-2 questions, offered a choice of what homework, assignments or tests they would like to do).
	    o Level 3 – Child engages in complete participation by actively partaking in the entire activity (e.g. asked questions, submitting all homework, assignments and tests).
	☐ Provide multiple opportunities to repeat and practise each level before moving to the next level.
	☐ Gradually increase child's level of participation in the task.
	☐ Consistently acknowledge, offer encouragement and positive reinforcement for participation at any level, any improvement, effort and displays of confidence made in the task.
	☐ Forewarn the child of any changes of activities, staff or locations.
	☐ Offer the choice to the child to participate or not in the changed schedule.

Supportive activities → Activity visuals, materials and resources

What?	Use a variety of activity visuals, materials and resources to enable the child to accomplish tasks successfully.
Why?	If a child perceives an activity as being too difficult, too easy, too demanding, too ambiguous or not meaningful, these triggers can contribute to the occurrence of challenging behaviours related to school refusal for a variety of functions (e.g. escape/avoid activity; gain/obtain adult interaction). To address these triggers, it is important to provide scaffolding. Scaffolding refers to the particular kind of help, assistance and techniques that enables a child to do a task which they cannot quite manage on their own and which brings them closer to a state of competence that will enable them to carry out other similar tasks independently in the future (Maybin, Mercer & Stierer, 1992).
	Visual scaffolding is the use of physical artefacts, visual strategies, graphic organisers, mind maps and visual media in conjunction with verbal speech. Visual scaffolding helps the child better understand the information, make connections, better express themselves, promotes self-learning, increases independence and decreases anxiety. This is especially useful when dealing with a child with difficulties in attention, communication and emotional regulation skills. Visuals allow the child access to the information at any time without having to depend on others to verbally remind them, but also replaces the demand being given by an adult which can sometimes add stress to a situation.
	By providing the activity materials it can help the child get on with participating in the activity instead of feeling frustrated or stalling because they have forgotten the material.
	Providing assistive technology i.e. any device, system or design that addresses the child's needs can enhance their capacity and motivation to perform tasks that might otherwise be difficult or impossible.
	By providing the necessary activity visuals, materials and assistive technology resources, the need for transitions and movement around the room can also be minimised.

How?	☐ Physical artefacts
	    o Models
	    o Real objects
	
	☐ Visual strategies
	    o Break card

- Daily schedule
- Task analysis
- Rules chart
- Materials checklist
- Instruction summary
- Reward system
- Free time activity choices
- Feelings chart
- Social story™
- Social script
- Comic strip conversations™
- Cause effect links

☐ Graphic organisers
- Cluster chart
- Fact-opinion chart
- 5 W's chart
- KWL chart
- Persuasion map
- Sequence chart
- Story map
- Venn diagram
- Activity scaffold

☐ Mind maps
- Flow map
- Multi-flow map
- Brace map
- Tree map
- Circle maps
- Bubble maps
- Double bubble maps
- Bridge map

☐ Visual media
- Computer games
- Series

	o Documentary
	  o Film
	  o Games
	  o Digital stories
	  o Apps
	
	☐ Extra activity materials for the child to borrow.
	☐ Resources to reduce auditory distractions like noise cancelling headphones and ear plugs.
	☐ Resources to help reduce visual distractions while working, such as workspace carrels, sparsely decorated areas and uncluttered activity areas.
	☐ Resources to address child's sensory needs (e.g. sensory diet, sensory space and sensory tools), communication needs (e.g. visual strategies, taped lectures and communication devices), learning needs (e.g. modified work, multisensory materials and spelling tools), hearing needs (e.g. modifying acoustical environment, front row seating and hearing devices), physical needs (e.g. mobility accessible environment, adjustable workstation and alternative keyboards), vision needs (e.g. magnifiers, text to speech software and Brailler).
	☐ Resources to create a digital or a physical portfolio containing a record of the tasks the child has completed that the child can refer to build confidence in their abilities.

Supportive activities → Activity design

What?	Design activities that alternate in their demands. Additionally, tailor activities and break-time activities to match the child's needs.
Why?	Creating such a schedule helps the child to learn effectively and progress. Children vary in their ability to cope with activity demands for a number of reasons e.g. ability to tolerate frustration, level of motivation, length of time they can pay attention, sense of competence to complete the activity, perceived meaningfulness and relevance of the activity. By creating a balanced schedule with tailored activities and reducing unstructured/idle time, opportunities are minimised for the child to go off task; which then requires some type of directive that creates the potential for a power struggle and frustration related to stopping a preferred activity. Also, providing the child with regular breaks helps them self-regulate, regain and maintain self-composure.
How?	☐ Create a balanced schedule for the child by tailoring activities to the child's abilities, interests and learning styles:

- Alternate between difficult and easy activities.
- Alternate between high and low interest tasks.
- Alternate between passive and active tasks.
- Ease transition from highly preferred activity to non-preferred activity by inserting a neutral or preferred activity in between.
- Insert highly stimulating activities in the daily schedule.
- Structure activities during unstructured times.
- Insert a calming activity before and after stressful activities to help the child stay calm.
- Insert activities in the daily schedule where the child has to help, give or do kind things for others.
- Identify and allocate the child jobs or responsibilities which they can complete successfully.
- Incorporate special interests and hobbies to increase motivation, engagement and participation in scheduled activities.
- Incorporate a reward system to keep the child motivated throughout the day.
- Incorporate prescribed sensory diet into their schedule especially at times in the day when challenging behaviours related to school refusal is most likely to occur.
- Insert a calming activity before and after stressful activities to help the child remain calm.
- Include stress reduction breaks in the schedule at regular intervals to help the child release tension, relax their body and avoid becoming frustrated. Break activities include drinking water, physical and relaxation exercises, singing and doing minimal challenge tasks.
- Throughout the day encourage the child to do heavy work and movement activities (e.g. jumping, pushing, lifting, carrying, climbing) for their calming and organising effect.

☐ Tailor activities to increase engagement by adjusting:
- Difficulty of the activity so that there is a high rate of correct response.
- Activity length so that there is a high rate of positive engagement and avoidance of fatigue.
- Purpose and appropriateness of the task.
- Order of learning.
- Waiting periods.
- Pace and way instruction is delivered to the child.
- Amount of information provided at one time.

	<ul><li>○ Complexity of the task.</li><li>○ Number of the items that the child is expected to learn.</li><li>○ How the child can respond to the task.</li><li>○ Time allowed for processing information, learning, task completion and testing.</li><li>○ Amount of support provided to child.</li><li>○ Number of opportunities provided to practise and develop the skill.</li><li>○ Activity start and finish time.</li><li>○ Time provided to transition to a new location or activity.</li></ul> ☐ Break activities down into small manageable steps/tasks/milestones. ☐ Use cooperative learning strategies to minimise competition in activities. ☐ Discuss the daily schedule with the child before commencing the day. ☐ Refer to the daily schedule at regular times throughout the day.

Supportive activities → Activity instruction

What?	Adapt the activity instruction method, reinforcement and management style to match the child's needs, abilities and preferences.
Why?	By making adaptations to the way instructions are provided, instruction related triggers that contribute to the challenging behaviours related to school refusal can be minimised or avoided. This can result in increased compliance and enable the child to successfully participate in the activity from the beginning to the end.
How?	☐ Before commencing the activity ensure all the necessary visual aids, materials and resources are available. ☐ Remove items that are not being used to eliminate unnecessary distractions. ☐ Create rules with the child to help them understand behavioural expectations for each context (i.e. what behaviour is allowed and not allowed). ☐ Review rules, expectations and aims before commencing the activity. ☐ Limit the number of adults supervising and facilitating the child's skill development at any one time. ☐ Use a consistent pattern for starting activities. ☐ Gain the child's attention before giving instruction. ☐ Speak in a varied tone, pitch, volume and inflection to emphasise and add interest. ☐ Be aware of rate, length and complexity of provided information. ☐ Maintain pace and flow by minimising time taken to present information.

- [ ] Use a combination of visual, auditory and kinaesthetic (hands-on) activities to support verbal instruction.
- [ ] Organise instructions in sequence.
- [ ] Give one instruction at a time.
- [ ] Avoid instruction phrased as a yes/no question because the child could refuse.
- [ ] Avoid instruction phrased with an OK at the end because the child could refuse.
- [ ] Avoid instruction phrased as a command, as the child could feel challenged or threatened.
- [ ] Phrase instructions as polite one-step requests by ending them with please or thankyou.
- [ ] Phrase instructions in 'first-then' format.
- [ ] Phrase instructions as request for help.
- [ ] Phrase instructions with two choices to guide the child's decision.
- [ ] Embed a fun and humorous instructional approach if appropriate.
- [ ] Deliver instruction and move away.
- [ ] Provide time to process.
- [ ] Provide extended time for compliance.
- [ ] Keep talking to a minimum as the child engages in the activity.
- [ ] Ask if the child needs assistance and offer help accordingly.
- [ ] Encourage the child to identify and correct own errors.
- [ ] Insert stress reduction breaks at the beginning, middle and end of activities to prevent the child from becoming frustrated
- [ ] Use private and discreet signals to remind the child to correct their behaviour and refocus on activity.
- [ ] Provide advance warning that the child will be called upon shortly.
- [ ] Prepare and provide explanations for any changes.
- [ ] Provide extra time and advance warnings to prepare the child for transitions by using countdowns and a finishing routine.
- [ ] Have a consistent pattern for ending activities.
- [ ] Ask the child to complete a behaviour reflection checklist to encourage self-evaluation, self-management and self-reinforcement skills.
- [ ] Have regular comprehension checkpoints when interacting to check the child's understanding of content and instructions.

Supportive interactions → Interaction to promote connection

What?	Actively facilitate the development of staff-child relationship and friendships to develop the child's sense of connection and belonging at school.
Why?	For a child who is returning after a long absence, the child may experience a range of emotions (e.g. anxiety, shame and feeling upset). Actively considering ways that help the child feel connected to staff and peers will encourage school attendance. It is important to get the child's input on how much engagement they would feel comfortable with and then over time the level of interaction can be increased.
How?	☐ Provide safe, inclusive and respectful school climates that addresses all forms of bullying, including cyberbullying. Before the child returns to school: ☐ Ask the child how they would like to be greeted by staff. ☐ Ask the child if they would like the teacher to ask them questions or ask if they need help. ☐ Ask where they would like to sit in the classroom and outside classroom activities (e.g. assemblies, excursions and other group activities). ☐ Encourage peers to greet and interact with the child. ☐ Organise seating arrangements to ensure supportive peers sit next to the child. ☐ Create a buddy system so that the child is paired with a buddy to assist with transitions to different classes and less structured situations. ☐ Encourage the child to participate in structured break time activities. ☐ Encourage the child to go to the library, office or student wellbeing centre if they are finding break times overwhelming or are feeling isolated. Schedule catch up sessions ☐ Initially schedule daily one-on-one meeting times with a staff member from the administration and/or well-being team. This will allow staff to gauge how the child is progressing and to build a relationship with staff. Gradually reduce the meetings to once a week. ☐ Begin the meeting by acknowledging how far the child has come and the importance of addressing any issues so that the child stays on track. ☐ In the meeting use a reflection sheet to gauge how the child is progressing, identify any concerns or difficulties and collaboratively brainstorm possible ways to address these difficulties.

Sample reflection sheet

A reflection sheet can be created to provide a structure to these meetings. The sheet can be completed with the child and their feedback can be shared with the team to make changes as necessary.

	Weekly Reflection Sheet	
Date	Timetable (tick subjects attended)	Any changes
		Environment related issues ☐ No ☐ Yes Seating in classroom ☐ No ☐ Yes Teacher instructions ☐ No ☐ Yes Lesson content ☐ No ☐ Yes Class participation ☐ No ☐ Yes Homework/tests/assignments ☐ No ☐ Yes Staff/peer related issues ☐ No ☐ Yes

How have I felt about this week?
☐ Green - Doing OK
☐ Orange - Not OK but coping
☐ Red- Not OK, not coping

Suggestions for changes to timetable for next week
☐ Increase number of subjects
☐ Decrease number of subjects
☐ Keep them the same
☐ Other

☐ Regularly monitor and review the effectiveness of the suggested strategies to determine if they are easing the child's concerns.

☐ Encourage the child to acknowledge and affirm the positives that have occurred at school.

Gratitude worksheet

The gratitude worksheet allows the child to record all the positive things they did for other people and positive things other people did for them; this helps to affirm a sense of purpose and happiness.

Gratitude worksheet

Child name _____ Date _____

What is something positive I did for others this week?
I helped:

- ☐ Teacher
- ☐ Class mate
- ☐ Visitor
- ☐ Other

I helped them:

- ☐ In an activity by
- ☐ Do a job by
- ☐ With their feelings by
- ☐ Other

How did I feel about helping?
What did the other person think about me helping them?

This week I was helped by:

- ☐ Teacher
- ☐ Class mate
- ☐ Visitor
- ☐ Other

They helped me:

- ☐ In an activity by
- ☐ Do a job by
- ☐ With their feelings by
- ☐ Other

How did I feel about them helping me?

Supportive interactions → Adult interaction

What?	Interact with the child in ways that demonstrate understanding, acceptance and responsiveness to the child's needs, abilities and preferences.
Why?	By consistently interacting in ways that are mindful of the child's needs, interaction related triggers that contribute to the challenging behaviours related to school refusal can be minimised or avoided. This will help the child feel valued, respected and supported, and lead to the establishment of trusting and healthy relationships.
How?	☐ Establish consistency in behavioural reactions, expectations and management strategies between adults. ☐ Get agreement on language that will be consistently used to give the child feedback. ☐ Be approachable and friendly. ☐ Demonstrate caring behaviour towards all children ☐ Show genuine interest in the child. ☐ Build a relationship by getting to know the child's interests, personality and background. ☐ Avoid making promises that are difficult to keep. ☐ Model empathy, self-control and positive social skills. ☐ Communicate high but realistic expectations to the child that can be enforced consistently. ☐ Do regular emotional check-ins to help child label and manage feelings and emotions in a healthy way. ☐ Provide the child with frequent verbal and non-verbal positive reinforcement for engaging in positive behaviours. ☐ Build understanding of relationship rights and responsibilities. ☐ Praise the child for following the rules. ☐ Consistently recognise the child's effort, participation and improvement in school attendance and participation. ☐ Provide child with choice-making opportunities. ☐ Strengthen the child's spirit, self-esteem and confidence by never shaming them. ☐ Provide four positive encouragement statements to one corrective statement. ☐ Acknowledge the child's positive contributions. ☐ Avoid bringing attention to differences between the child and peers. ☐ Avoid situations or talking about topics with the child that can cause conflict. ☐ Avoid being drawn into arguments, bargaining or excuses with the child.

	☐ Avoid taking what the child says or does personally.
	☐ Indicate what is agreed with, state position clearly and walk away.
	☐ Discuss things calmly, briefly and privately.

Supportive interactions → Peer interaction

What?	Support positive child–peer interaction so that relationships can be built and successful teamwork can be achieved.
Why?	Some children with SRB have difficulties with social interaction (e.g. initiate and maintain friendships, resolve conflicts and communicate in an assertive manner). Children with social difficulties are at risk of being socially isolated and rejected by their peers and experiencing low self-esteem, thus further exacerbating the situation.
How?	☐ Be mindful of how groups are organised, seated and number of children in an activity. ☐ Reduce access to peers who are likely to cause problems for the child. ☐ Reduce access to peers that the child victimises. ☐ Intervene, redirect and provide peer mediation to manage disputes. ☐ Educate peers about the child's needs. ☐ Seat the child next to a peer study buddy who can help maintain attention. ☐ Use a buddy system to help the child develop social relationships especially during recess and/or lunch.

Supportive interactions → Teach skills

What?	Use direct, explicit and systematic teaching when the child is calm to provide the child with multiple opportunities to learn skills by: 1. discussing the importance of the skill, modelling the skill, 2. providing guided practise to coach the child on how to use the skill in staged situations that simulate the actual situation and 3. using the skill in a variety of contexts independently.
Why?	By helping the child learn the appropriate alternative behaviour to deal with the triggers/problems, the child's need to resort to challenging behaviours associated with SRB can be minimised or avoided. Below are examples of the skills that can be targeted.
How?	☐ Teach skills for successful participation: ☐ Cognitive Skills

- Attention skills (e.g. orient, focus, select, maintain and shift attention).
- Memory skills (e.g. encode, store, retain and recall information).
- Thinking skills (e.g. problem solve, make decisions, ask questions, construct plans, evaluate ideas, and create new ideas).
- Executive functioning skills (e.g. plan, organise, sequence, monitor one's performance, utilise feedback, inhibit inappropriate response, being flexible, time management skills and self-regulation skills).

☐ Physical skills
- Gross motor skills (e.g. jump, climb and run).
- Fine motor skills (e.g. eat, write, cut, construct, tie, paste, turn, open, squeeze, button, pour, paint and hold things).

☐ Communication skills
- Receptive skills (e.g. understand routines, words, phrases, instructions, directions, questions and concepts).
- Expressive skills (e.g. request/reject affection, objects, action, information, assistance, clarification, attention; making choices and sharing information).

☐ Social skills
- Non-verbal social communication skills (e.g. eye contact, facial expression, gestures, body language, private vs. public behaviour, proximity, volume, and listening).
- Verbal social communication skills (e.g. greet others, gain attention, asking for help, initiate/maintain/end conversations, assertive communication, share jokes, join a group, work co-operatively and make friends).
- Play skills (e.g. sharing, turn-taking, waiting and engaging in different types of play).
- Emotional regulation skills (i.e. identify, understand, regulate and work through one's own emotions; read, comprehend and empathise with emotional states in others).
- Self-concept, self-esteem and self-efficacy skills.

☐ Teach the child independence skills by targeting activity steps the child needs to learn and gradually fading prompts and supports.

☐ Teach about the growth mindset where frustrations, mistakes and failures are seen as opportunities to learn something new, gain a new skill and grow.

	☐ Use behavioural contracts to help the child understand goal/expectations, consequences and rewards for compliance.
	☐ Use tangible, edible, sensory, social and activity rewards to motivate the child to work towards their goal.

Supportive environments → Physical environment

What?	Purposefully arrange the environment in ways that are responsive to the needs of the child and help the child feel safe and calm in the classroom.
Why?	Providing an organised, predictable and distraction-free environment can help the child feel safe, in control and regulated. Providing the child with a calm down area that they can access regularly can help the child maintain their emotional control and/or regain emotional composure and not escalate.
How?	☐ Create a clutter free and organised environment by using labelled storage systems to store materials. ☐ Create a sensory friendly environment. ☐ Set up the environment to provide maximum personal space for everyone. ☐ Identify a quiet learning area where the child can go to complete work or do a test. ☐ Allocate a calm down area inside or outside the classroom. ☐ Provide calming activities (e.g. Lego, colouring in, drawing, putty and puzzles) in the calm down area.

Supportive environments → Positioning in environment

What?	Position the child in the environment in ways that are responsive to their needs.
Why?	Considered positioning of the child in the environment can minimise or avoid triggers that contribute to the SRB by instead enabling them to focus, develop skills and stay on task.
How?	☐ Seat the child in the classroom based on their preference. ☐ Position the child next to peers who are good role models. ☐ Position the child away from noise generating areas. ☐ Position the child in an area with minimal auditory distractions. ☐ Position the child in an area with minimal visual distractions. ☐ Position the child in an area with minimal traffic flow. ☐ Position the child in an area with minimal distracting smells.

Supportive environments → Environmental routines

What?	Create and practice routines that help the child move around the environment in a smooth, efficient and organised manner.
Why?	Providing the child with multiple opportunities to practice the steps involved in transitioning between activities, people and locations can help the child learn how to carry them out as independently as possible.
How?	☐ Establish and follow routine consistently. ☐ Establish and practise routines for entering and leaving the environment. ☐ Establish and practise routines for getting ready for the activity. ☐ Establish and practise routines for collecting materials and resources. ☐ Establish and practise routines for moving around in the environment. ☐ Establish and practise routines for waiting. ☐ Establish and practise routines for transitioning between environments.

Prevent Plan Form

Child name _____ Date _____

Recorder name/s _____

Suggested re-entry steps Target re-entry step discussed in this plan Target re-entry step estimated time period Review date for target re-entry step progress	
Strategies for supportive activities	
Strategies for supportive interactions	
Teach skills	
Strategies for supportive environments	

8. CONCLUSION

SRB is the result of a complex combination of factors so a team approach that includes the caregivers, school, professionals and other community agencies is required to address SRB.

At the school level there are a range of strategies that can be utilised to support the team.

If the SRB has been occurring for a while, it is not going to disappear overnight. It is important to consider that each child is different and the length of time spent on each step will depend on the child. This is not a race and speed is not the answer! Change is also not a linear process, often it involves taking a step forward and a few steps backwards. This is part of the journey.

The journey of behavioural change is a cyclic, ongoing process that consists of three stages: Assess – Manage - Prevent. The first step of the journey is to Assess in order to understand the message (function) that the child is communicating through the SRB, and then to develop a Management and Prevention plan.

Once the plan is implemented it is important to evaluate the effectiveness of the Manage and Prevent stages by repeating the Assess stage to measure the amount or type of progress that has been made. This can help you determine the effectiveness of the Manage and Prevent strategies and refine and adapt them to ultimately help the child reach their full potential.

Please remember while SRB may not disappear overnight, with persistence, patience and perseverance, the child can gradually learn positive ways of behaving and managing their emotions.

9. REFERENCES

- Allison, M. & Attisha, E. (2019). The Link Between School Attendance and Good Health. *Paediatrics, 143*, 1-13.

- American Psychiatric Association (2013). *Diagnostic and Statistical Manual of Mental Disorders (5th Ed.).* Arlington, VA: American Psychiatric Publishing.

- Barry, A. E., Chaney, B., & Chaney, J. (2011). The impact of truant and alcohol-related behavior on educational aspirations: A study of us high school seniors. *Journal of School Health, 8*, 485-492.

- Boivin, M., Hymel, S. & Bukowski, W.M. (1995). The roles of social withdrawal, peer rejection and victimization by peers in predicting loneliness and depressed mood in childhood. *Development and Psychopathology, 7*, 765–85.

- British Columbia School Superintendents' Association (2011). *Supporting Students with Learning Disabilities: A Guide for Teachers.* Victoria, B.C.: Ministry of Education. Accessed on the 7th of October 2020 http://www.llbc.leg.bc.ca/public/pubdocs/bcdocs2011_2/498894/learning_disabilities_guide.pdf

- Bukowski, W.M., & Adams, R. (2005). Peer relationships and psychopathology: markers, moderators, mediators, mechanisms and meanings. *Journal of Clinical Child & Adolescent Psychology, 34*, 3-10.

- Department of Education Queensland (2011). *A guide for bus and taxi drivers of students with special needs.* State of Queensland: Department of Transport and Main Roads.

- Rainey, L., Elsman, E.B.M., Van Nispen, R.M.A., Van Leeuwen, L.M., & Van Rens, G.H.M.B. (2016). Comprehending the impact of low vision on the lives of children and adolescents: A qualitative approach. *Quality of Life Research, 25*, 2633 – 2643.

- Flakierska-Praquin N., Lindstrom M., Gillberg C. (1997). School phobia with separation anxiety disorder: a comparative 20- to 29-year follow-up study of 35 school refusers. *Comprehensive Psychiatry, 38,* 17-22.

- Fremont, W. (2003). School refusal in children and adolescents. *American Family Physician,* 68,1555–64.

- Gazelle, H.& Ladd, G.W.(2003). Anxious solitude and peer exclusion: a diathesis-stress model of internalizing trajectories in childhood. *Child Development, 74,* 257–78.

- Gonzálvez, C., Ingles, C., Kearney, C., Sanmartín, R., Vicent J. M., García-Fernández, J. (2019). Relationship between school refusal behavior and social functioning: a cluster analysis approach. *European Journal of Education and Psychology, 12,* 17-29.

- Gubbels, J., van der Put, C.E., & Assink, M. (2019) Risk Factors for School Absenteeism and Dropout: A Meta-Analytic Review. *Journal of Youth and Adolescence, 48,* 1637–1667.

- Henry, K. L., & Thornberry, T. P. (2010). Truancy and escalation of substance use during adolescence. *Journal of Studies on Alcohol & Drugs, 71,* 115-124.

- Heyne, D., King, N.J., Tonge, B. & Cooper, H. (2002). School refusal: description and management. *Current Therapeutics, 43,* 55-61.

- Heyne, D., King, N.J., Tonge, B. & Cooper, H. (2001). School refusal: epidemiology and management. *Paediatric Drugs, 3,* 719-32.

- Kawsar, M.D.S, Yilanli M. & Marwaha, R. (2020). School Refusal. Accessed on the 12th of September 2020 from https://www.ncbi.nlm.nih.gov/books/NBK534195/

- Kearney, C. A. (2001). *School refusal behavior in youth: A functional approach to assessment and treatment.* American Psychological Association.

- Kearney, C. A. (2008). An interdisciplinary model of school absenteeism in youth to inform professional practice and public policy. *Educational Psychology Review, 20,* 257– 82.

- Kearney, C. A., & Silverman, W. K. (1996). The evolution and reconciliation of taxo-

- nomic strategies for school refusal behavior. *Clinical Psychology: Science and Practice, 3*, 339–354.

- Kearney, C.A., Cook, L.C., & Chapman, G. (2007). School stress and school refusal behavior. In G. Fink (Ed.), *Encyclopedia of stress* (2nd ed., Vol. 3, pp. 422-425). San Diego, CA: Academic Press.

- Klass, C.S., Guskin, K.A., & Thomas, M. (1995). The early childhood program: Promoting children's development through and within relationships. *Zero to Three 16,* 9–17.

- Lyon, A.R. & Colter, S. (2007). Toward Reduced Bias and Increased Utility in the Assessment of School Refusal Behaviour: The Case for Diverse Samples and Evaluations of Context. *Psychology in the Schools, 44,* 551-565.

- McShane G., Walter G., & Rey, J.M. (2001). Characteristics of adolescents with school refusal. *Australian and New Zealand Journal of Psychiatry, 35,* 822–826.

- Mogensen, D. & Yiu, L. (2016). *Understanding Eating Disorders in BC Schools: A Guide of Trauma Informed Practices for School Professionals.* Accessed on the 12th of September 2020 from https://keltyeatingdisorders.ca/wp-content/uploads/2016/06/Understanding-Eating-Disorders-in-Schools.pdf

- Ohio Department of Education. (2002). *What Is a Functional Behavior Assessment? The "WHY" of a Behavior.* Columbus, OH.

- Place, M., Hulsmeier, J., Davis, S., & Taylor, E. (2002). The coping mechanisms of children with school refusal. *Journal of Research in Special Educational Needs, 2,* 1–10.

- Prizant, B. M., Wetherby, A. M., Rubin, E., Laurent, A. C., & Rydell, P. J. (2006). *The SCERTS Model: A comprehensive educational approach for children with autism spectrum disorders: Volume II program planning & intervention.* Baltimore: Paul H. Brookes.

- Rainey, L., Elsman, E.B.M., Van Nispen, R.M.A., Van Leeuwen, L.M., & Van Rens G.H.M.B. (2016). Comprehending the impact of low vision on the lives of children and adolescents: A qualitative approach. *Quality of Life Research, 25,* 2633 – 2643.

- Setzer, N. & Salzhauer, A. (2001). *Understanding School Refusal.* NYU Child Study Center.

- Sewell J. (2008). School refusal. *Australian Family Physician, 37,* 406-8.

- Wijetunge, G.S. & Lakmini, W.D., (2011). School refusal in children and adolescents. *Sri Lanka Journal of Child Health, 40,* 128–131

APPENDIX:
BEHAVIOUR HELP WEB-BASED APP

Step by step guide to assessing-managing-preventing challenging behaviour

Who can use the Behaviour Help web-based app?

The Behaviour Help web-based app is a valuable tool for parents, childcare centres, preschools, primary/secondary schools, disability services, child and youth services ... anyone supporting individuals with emotional and behavioural difficulties.

What is unique about the Behaviour Help web-based app?

The Behaviour Help web-based app provides a bank of evidence-based, practical ideas, strategies and suggestions for the assessment, escalation profiling, management and prevention of emotional and behavioural difficulties. As a team of parents, caregivers, educators and professionals, you can select the ideas, strategies and suggestions that are appropriate and customise them to suit the child. Additionally, this printed guide contains many more ideas customised for the specific behavioural problem 'School Refusal Behaviour'. You can enter the relevant items, and even your own ideas, in the app. The software will put together a ready-to-print customised pdf behaviour Assessment, Intervention and Management Plan to help you transform the life of the child you support. This pdf document can then be shared with the team. The app allows you to update the documents as often as needed and digitally store all the behaviour support plans in the one place.

How many children can I use the Behaviour Help web-based app with?

You can create as many profiles on the app as you wish.

What devices can the Behaviour Help web-based app be used on?

Behaviour Help is a web-based app that can be used on your Mac or PC, or on a tablet.

How do I access the Behaviour Help web-based app?

Please visit www.behaviourhelp.com/app/#/signup.

ABOUT THE AUTHOR

Hi there,

I am Dolly Bhargava. I have completed a Bachelor of Applied Science in Speech Pathology from the University of Sydney, a Master of Special Education from the University of Newcastle, and Certificate IV in Training and Assessment.

Midway through my career I realised my passion was in supporting children, adolescents and adults with emotional and behavioural difficulties (EBD). So I started working extensively with individuals with EBD in a variety of contexts such as family homes, childcare centres, preschool, schools, respite care, post school options, employment services and corrective services.

I have created this series based on the practical wisdom I have gathered from working with individuals with EBD, their families, educators and professionals over the last 21 years. I hope this guide equips people with the knowledge, skills and tools to help your child learn positive ways of behaving and managing their emotions.

Dolly Bhargava

www.ingramcontent.com/pod-product-compliance
Lightning Source LLC
Chambersburg PA
CBHW080637230426
43663CB00016B/2903